MY DAD *wished* HE HAD ONE OF THOSE

RICHARD PORTER & GILES CHAPMAN

HODDER &
STOUGHTON

First published in Great Britain in 2008 by Hodder & Stoughton
An Hachette Livre UK company

1

Copyright © Richard Porter and Giles Chapman 2008

The right of Richard Porter and Giles Chapman to be identified as the
Authors of the Work has been asserted by them in accordance with
the Copyright, Designs and Patents Act 1988.

A CIP catalogue record for this title is available from the British Library

ISBN 9780340 963241

Typeset and design by Craig Burgess in Adobe Caslon, Aurea and Futura

Printed and bound by L.E.G.O. Spa in Italy

Hodder & Stoughton policy is to use papers that are natural, renewable and
recyclable products and made from wood grown in sustainable forests. The
logging and manufacturing processes are expected to conform to the
environmental regulations of the country of origin.

Hodder & Stoughton Ltd
338 Euston Road
London NW1 3BH

www.hodder.co.uk

★ Contents

For Pieter Venema, Giles's father-in-law, for all his stamina-giving encouragement.

Richard would like to dedicate this book to Jules for her patience, her support and her grilled cheese sandwiches.

★ Introduction

Just because your Dad drove around in a Cortina or Marina or some other slice of four door, family-friendly, automotive white bread didn't mean he wasn't lusting after something longer, lower, more powerful and a whole lot sexier.

Take away the kids, the mortgage payments, your Mum's more practical desire for a kitchen extension and in his head he'd be there in the rakish supercar thundering towards Geneva, or reclining in a muscular roadster on the Côte d'Azur, the wind whipping through what was left of his hair.

With this book we wanted to celebrate the shiny metal dreams that occupied your Dad's idle moments. And because cars don't die, get relegated, put on weight, lose their looks or go stark staring mental and move into a mansion full of cats, to this very day Dad can dream about making them a part of his life.

MILK TRAY MAN

Alfa Romeo Montreal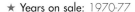

Like many great dream cars, the Alfa Montreal started life as a one-off, a concept car to ooze sex across a show stand. In this case, the show was Expo '67 in Canada, and for some reason Alfa was the only car maker invited to attend. Anyway, with the burden of representing the entire motor industry sitting upon their stylishly clothed shoulders, Alfa asked top Italian designer Bertone to come up with a unique design to wow the Canadian crowds, and this is the beauty they delivered, named after the city where it would be shown off.

Clearly far too gorgeous to be locked in a Milanese warehouse, Alfa decided to make a go of it, turning the one-off into something you could actually buy. The styling stayed the same but the engine, a weedy four cylinder in the show car, became a rampant V8 nicked from Alfa's racing department, and this, unfortunately, turned out to be the Montreal's downfall. It was just too highly strung and, when the fuel crisis hit in the early '70s, its insatiable appetite for juice killed sales dead.

Still, in later years it achieved a Dad-tastic fantasy double whammy when model Yasmin Le Bon bought one, proving that her taste in cars was better than her taste in husbands.

★ **Years on sale:** 1970-77
★ **Engine:** V8 cylinder, fuel-injected, 2593cc, mounted at the front
★ **Bodywork:** two-door, two-seater coupé
★ **Top speed:** 137mph
★ **0-60mph acceleration time:** 7.6sec
★ **Maximum power:** 200bhp
★ **Original price:** £5077 (in 1972)

Connoisseur's choice or poverty pick? There's just the one model, so it's take the Montreal with all its fabulousness and foibles, or leave it.

> **FACT: When it went on sale in Britain, the Montreal cost more than a Jaguar E-type. Ouch.**

Aston Martin DBS/V8

The Aston Martin DB5 (and its near-identical successor, the DB6) are forever linked with Sean Connery's James Bond. And there are a lot of similarities. Both were suave, powerful, handsome, and cooler than a polar bear's paws. Both were also rather hard to replace, and when the DB6 was superseded by this, the DBS, there was palpable disappointment. The elegance, the grace, the subtle but simmering aggression seemed to have been lost somehow. This was the George Lazenby of Astons. Little wonder then that Lazenby's Bond drove a DBS in *On Her Majesty's Secret Service*. And, like the least popular 007 (after Timothy Dalton), the DBS was unfairly slated.

Certainly, it didn't perform as well as it should have done, being heavier than the DB6 but using the same six-cylinder engine because its new V8 wasn't ready, but in all other respects it was far more modern than the car it replaced. Even the smart four-headlamp grille that so horrified Aston anoraks looks rather groovy now.

Aston Martin, however, weren't so sure, and in 1972 the DBS was given an effective nip-and-tuck job that brought back a more traditional grille. In this form it showed amazing longevity, staying current until the end of the 1980s and remaining highly sought after to this day. Unlike George Lazenby.

★ **Years on sale:** 1967-90
★ **Engine:** straight-six cylinder, triple-carburettor, 3995cc/V8 cylinder, triple-carburettor or fuel-injected, 5340cc, mounted at the front
★ **Bodywork:** two-door, two-seater coupé
★ **Top speed:** 140mph (DBS)/162mph (V8)
★ **0-60mph acceleration time:** 7.1sec (DBS)/6sec (V8)
★ **Maximum power:** 282bhp (DBS)/never stated (V8)
★ **Original price:** £5500 (DBS in 1967)/ £6897 (V8 in 1972)

Connoisseur's choice or poverty pick? After years in the V8's shadow, the straight-six DBS is now keenly sought, especially if it has the rare Vantage engine with another 43bhp on tap.

> **FACT: Roger Moore drove a DBS in gentlemen-go-around-punching-people TV series The Persuaders. His was a six-cylinder car, re-trimmed to look like the manlier V8 model.**

Fiat Dino

Under normal circumstances a Fiat is not the sort of car to figure in some '60s daydream about thundering across the Alps for a rendezvous with your mythical Italian mistress. It's more the kind of weedy snot box you'd be given by a rental company to grind your way over the mountains for a conference about plastic fixatives. But the Dino was no ordinary Fiat, because its genes came straight from Ferrari. So, this was a car with the badge of a donkey but the heart of a thoroughbred.

Ferrari, having made an uncharacteristically tiny V6 for Formula Two racing, needed to homologate the engine in at least 500 road cars. Not wanting to sully themselves with making such a number of street machines with half the cylinders of their normal stock-in-trade, they made a call to their chums at Fiat who were happy to concoct what, for them, would be a high-glamour, top-of-the-range sports car. Or rather, a pair of sports cars, because the Dino came in two distinct forms: a coupé designed by Torinese coachbuilder Bertone, or a roadster created by their rivals at Pininfarina, the latter turning out so beautiful that it made you want to lick it.

Sadly, the 2-litre engine was less demure. In fact, it was so unruly Fiat was eventually forced to solve its reliability problems by junking

it and starting again with a 2.4 V6. But that really wasn't the point. Yes, Ferrari might have stiffed them with an engine that didn't really work properly, but without that original deal Fiat would never have had a flagship as truly, madly, deeply gorgeous as this.

★ **Years on sale:** 1966-73
★ **Engine:** V6 cylinder, triple-carburettor, 1987/2418cc, mounted at the front
★ **Bodywork:** two-door, 2+2 coupé or two-door, two-seater roadster
★ **Top speed:** 130mph (2400 Coupé)
★ **0-60mph acceleration time:** 8.1sec (2000 Coupé)
★ **Maximum power:** 180bhp (2400)
★ **Original price:** £3493 (2400 Coupé in 1970)

Connoisseur's choice or poverty pick? The ratio of Coupés to Spiders built is four-to-one, making the Pininfarina-built soft top even more desirable. That said, a 2400 Coupé is extremely stylish. No right-hand drive, by the way.

> **FACT:** The Mafia bosses in The Italian Job drove black Fiat Dinos. The sinister coupé, rather than the not-as-scary-looking roadster, of course.

Fiat 130 Coupé

The Fiat 130 saloon was an unexceptional large car, seemingly designed solely for high-ranking Italian civil servants so they had something nice in which to ride and – this being '70s Italy – eventually get shot or blown up. The 130 Coupé, however, was an entirely different kettle of ball games.

It's pretty clear that the key instrument in most 1970s car designs was the ruler, but the two-door 130 showed that an era-specific allergy to curves wasn't always a barrier to making a beautiful car, because the masters at design house Pininfarina managed to give it a body to die for. The interior was rather special too, especially since parts of the dashboard appeared to be made from the same sort of wood that you'd find wrapped around a top-notch '70s tuner-amp.

In the hands of some car makers, the sum total of a protractor-phobic exterior and ultra-brown interior could have been vile, but Fiat, with that fine Italian sense of detail and proportion, just made it stick. Unfortunately what they couldn't make stick was the idea of a Casino Square car wearing a Benidorm badge, and the 130

Coupé was rare as a result, getting more and more exclusive as time went on and owners discovered just how quickly its fast-corroding bodywork turned to dust. Still, in keeping with the general '70s-ness of the whole car, at least the rust spots would have been brown.

★ **Years on sale:** 1971-77
★ **Engine:** V6 cylinder, single-carburettor, 3235cc, mounted at the front
★ **Bodywork:** two-door, four-seater coupé
★ **Top speed:** 116mph
★ **0-60mph acceleration time:** 10.6sec
★ **Maximum power:** 165bhp
★ **Original price:** £5609 (in 1973)

Connoisseur's choice or poverty pick? You can enjoy that magnificent V6 engine – designed by Ferrari's Aurelio Lampredi – at a fraction of the cost in the 130 saloon. But it shares none of the Coupé's stunning looks.

> **FACT: Dusty Springfield owned a 130 Coupé with – proto-bling alert! – gold-plated door handles.**

Jaguar XJ-S

Proof, if it were needed, that the 1970s were really quite bonkers comes with this often-maligned grand tourer, which replaced the legendary Jaguar E-type. Even in its later life as a softer, V12-powered, gin-sodden cruiser, the E-type was gorgeous enough to make your mouth go dry. Whereas its replacement seemed only to fill it with bile.

The weird oval headlamps, the saggy-looking back lights, the bizarre buttresses either side of the rear window; all of them melded into a startling whole that instantly repelled E-type customers and almost anyone who had the gift of sight. The dark and simple interior didn't help, offering people stark modernism when what they wanted was a lavish cocoon made entirely of cow and tree.

Jag eventually fitted such luxury trimmings and, as befits a car that was always a bit cheesy, the XJ-S matured and grew in flavour to the point where it became an acceptable object of lust for dads

everywhere. In fact, even early XJ-Ss look quite saucy today, notwithstanding the bright '70s paint that many came in because the factory cocked up and for months could only build cars in three colours, one of which was yellow. The XJ-S's time has come, proving, if anything, that Jag's idea of a modern sports car just overshot the mark by about 30 years.

★ **Years on sale:** 1975-96
★ **Engine:** straight-six cylinder, fuel-injected, 3590-3980cc/V12 cylinder, fuel-injected, 5343-5994cc, mounted at the front
★ **Bodywork:** two-door, 2+2 coupé, two-door, two-seater cabriolet and two-seater and 2+2 convertible
★ **Top speed:** 150mph (XJR-S 6.0)
★ **0-60mph acceleration time:** 7.1sec (XJR-S 6.0)
★ **Maximum power:** 318bhp (XJR-S 6.0)
★ **Original price:** £8990 (V12 in 1975)

Connoisseur's choice or poverty pick? Jaguar's V12, which was axed in 1997, is one of the world's great engines, and makes the XJ-S an awesome continent-crossing GT; a late 1980s convertible example is best.

> **FACT:** In the early '70s a car journalist and his photographer were left alone within Jaguar HQ and stumbled upon an XJ-S prototype. The snapper prepared to bag a scoop until the journo told him not to bother since, 'Jaguar would never build anything that ugly.'

Jensen Interceptor

When it comes to making a dream car, the most important thing to get right isn't the performance or the handling or the gadgetry. It's the name. And here we have a case in point. Interceptor. Just hearing it makes you want to shout 'RAAAAAA!' or fantasise about a circumstance in which you could bark, 'Count Von Stromboli's getting away. Quick! To the Interceptor!'

The other thing to get right with a dream car is the styling and here, once again, the Jensen scored mightily. Its looks weren't entirely conventional, but with that huge bonnet and unusually stubby, glassy tail, it was a car that permanently appeared to be relaxing on a chaise longue. It was louche and decadent and somehow a bit naughty.

But though the design may have looked laid-back, the walloping Chrysler V8 up front – packing a whole 7.2 litres in later versions – meant the Interceptor had surprising brutality, like being unexpectedly punched in the face by Dean Martin. Sure, that rumbling engine sucked up fuel like it had a sponge cylinder

block, but in many ways that just added to its attraction as Dad imagined a time when he might be rich enough not only to buy an Interceptor but also to laugh in the face of its immense running costs. This car was, quite simply, the coolest thing ever to come out of West Bromwich.

★ **Years on sale:** 1966-76, 1984-1991
★ **Engine:** V8 cylinder, triple-carburettor, 5898-7212cc, mounted at the front
★ **Bodywork:** two-door, four-seater coupé; two-door, four-seater convertible
★ **Top speed:** 126mph (SP)
★ **0-60mph acceleration time:** 7.6sec (SP)
★ **Maximum power:** 330bhp (SP)
★ **Original price:** £3743 (Interceptor I in 1966)

Connoisseur's choice or poverty pick? There were only 267 convertibles and they're where the Interceptor big bucks lie. But it lacks the iconic glass fastback of the standard car, of which the Series II is probably the best all-rounder, fiery SP model notwithstanding.

> **FACT: The Interceptor spawned a version called the FF which was the first sports car to feature four-wheel drive and anti-lock brakes.**

IF DAD
WENT MAD

Alfa Romeo SZ

If your dad genuinely wished for one of these you might have asked your mother to change the dosage on his medication. It was a truly extraordinary-looking thing, its appearance rattling the refined and delicate tastes of the Italian media so much that they instantly branded it Il Mostro, meaning 'the monster'. Which, on reflection, seems a little unkind. Yes, the SZ – it stood for 'Sprint Zagato', after the Italian design house that built the car – was undoubtedly nutty, what with its extreme wedge shape, squinty six-headlight face and dramatically curved windscreen, but its pugnacious lumpiness was also weirdly captivating, like a photo of a defeated boxer with his eyes all bloodied and swollen.

Underneath the unusual body, the SZ was based on the somewhat less mentalist Alfa 75 saloon, but this was no bad thing since it meant a 3-litre V6 engine that made a nicer noise than most boy bands, and a gearbox mounted at the back, improving the weight distribution and making the SZ scoot round corners like a racing car. And with just over 1000 SZs made it had rarity on its

side as well. All in all, they might have called this car a monster, but it was actually quite sweet. A little bit like Shrek. Or Joan Rivers.

- ★ **Years on sale:** 1989-91
- ★ **Engine:** V6 cylinder, fuel-injected, 2959cc, mounted at the front
- ★ **Bodywork:** two-door, two-seater coupé
- ★ **Top speed:** 153mph
- ★ **0-60mph acceleration time:** 6.9sec
- ★ **Maximum power:** 210bhp
- ★ **Original price:** £40,000 (in 1989)

Connoisseur's choice or poverty pick? There's just the one type and spec although, if the SZ just isn't, erm, distinctive enough for you, there was also an open version, the RZ. With only 241 made, it's hyper-rare.

> **FACT: The SZ's odd looks were created by a chap called Robert Opron, who also designed another member of Mad Dad's fantasy garage, the Citroën SM.**

Citroën SM

An oval steering wheel; panels made from aircraft-grade aluminium; self-levelling oleopneumatic suspension; fully hydraulic power steering; headlamps that automatically levelled and turned to point in the direction you were going.

These are things that would be thought pretty avant-garde even today, but on a car announced in 1970 they were absolutely extraordinary. Frankly, it would have seemed no less plausible if Dad was actually lusting after a space rocket and a three-bed semi on the moon. But this was the sort of high-tech stuff that Citroën had specialised in ever since the wildly futuristic DS saloon of 1955, and for their new sporting flagship they really had gone all out to laden it with mind-blowing levels of sophistication. And, after buying Maserati in 1968, the French futurologists had an appropriately exotic engine for their new coupé too. It was a zinging 2.7-litre V6 which, as it turned out, had a nasty habit of going ping as well as zing.

This flakiness, along with the SM's massive complexity, didn't do good things for Citroën's bank balance, and in 1974 the

company went bust, allowing Peugeot to move in and take over. Under the new and fiscally prudent owners, the slow-selling SM was soon for the chop. Ironically, the car so far ahead of its time was killed off before the rest of the world had caught up.

* **Years on sale:** 1970-75
* **Engine:** V6 cylinder, triple-carburettor, 2670cc/fuel-injected, 2974cc, mounted at the front
* **Bodywork:** two-door, four-seater coupé
* **Top speed:** 142mph (3-litre)
* **0-60mph acceleration time:** 8.3sec (3-litre)
* **Maximum power:** 178bhp (3-litre)
* **Original price:** £5480 (2.7-litre in 1972)

Connoisseur's choice or poverty pick? Later fuel-injected engine is probably preferable but any SM is a wheeled wonder.

FACT: The SM enjoyed a bizarrely broad roster of famous owners, including racing driver Mike Hailwood, writer Graham Greene, Soviet president Leonid Brezhnev and murderous despot Idi Amin.

Ford GT40

Some basic facts about one of the most iconic racing cars ever made: it was fruit of Henry Ford II's desire to go endurance racing and, urban legend has it, built out of sheer bloody-mindedness after he tried to buy Ferrari, only for the Italians to back out at the last minute. It duly gave Enzo's boys a damn good drubbing on the track, coming home first, second and third at the 1966 Le Mans 24 Hours race. And, though originally called the GT, it acquired the rest of its name because it was a dwarfish 40 inches tall.

Those are the endlessly repeatedly headlines, but they don't entirely explain why Dad would have so lusted after one. You see, you could actually buy a GT40 for the road, making it seem tantalisingly within reach, and the road car was basically the victorious racer, lightly civilised with an exhaust silencer, softer shock absorbers, road-spec brakes and the choice of 150 paint colours in lieu of its track brethren's stickers and stripes. To all intents and purposes this was a 335-horsepower, Le Mans winning racer you could drive to the pub.

If that got Dad salivating, delving into the buying process would have had him drowning in his own juices because Ford asked that each GT40 buyer come to their HQ to be measured up for their car's seat and to choose the gearbox ratios. Speccing up your own GT40 sounded even more exciting than watching it win at Le Mans – which it did again in 1967, '68 and '69. There was, however, one big problem. Or rather, one problem for the big. Since the GT40 was so low, if you were a bit on the tall side you simply wouldn't fit. Hence, Richard E. Grant has never owned a GT40 whereas microscopic box-opener Noel Edmonds has.

★ **Years on sale:** 1966-68
★ **Engine:** V8 cylinder, single-carburettor, 4727cc, mounted in the centre
★ **Bodywork:** two-door, two-seater coupé
★ **Top speed:** 154mph (in road trim)
★ **0-60mph acceleration time:** 5.1sec
★ **Maximum power:** 335bhp
★ **Original price:** £6450 (MkIII in 1966)

Connoisseur's choice or poverty pick? There were 107 GT40s, mostly built as racecars but with all 31 of the MkIIIs sold in a detuned road-going specification. All have colossal value today.

> **FACT: When Ford announced a reinvented version of the GT40 in 2002 they realised they'd foolishly sold the name to a company that built replica GT40s. And which wanted a fortune to sell it back. Hence, the new car was called simply the Ford GT.**

Lancia Stratos

It looks like one of those insanely styled Hot Wheels cars, all cartoonishly swollen wheel arches and improbably curved windscreen, but the Lancia Stratos was far from a toy. In a time when car makers went rallying with modified saloons, the Stratos was the world's first machine purpose-built for the job.

It came about after Italian coachbuilder Bertone created a one-off show car which, since it required its passengers to get in through a hinged windscreen, made the actual Stratos look positively sensible. What this loon car did, however, was float the idea of a Lancia with its engine in the middle. The company's motorsport boss like this, and set about turning it into a rally weapon. As a bonus, Ferrari was about to kill off the Dino sports car and, after a bit of hand waving and shouting, agreed to let Lancia have its redundant V6 engine. The Stratos was ready to go.

Except, as it turned out, it wasn't, because in its first competitive rally the prototype's suspension collapsed. Ooops. Nonetheless, the Stratos went on to monster the rally championship throughout the mid- and late '70s. But what made it truly exciting was that under rallying rules 500 road-going cars had to be built. So, if he could find

the cash – but not his marbles – Dad could have bought a Stratos of his own. Obviously it would have been claustrophobic, impossibly hot, incredibly hard to drive, and prone to spinning out of control, but that wasn't the point.

- ★ **Years on sale:** 1973-75
- ★ **Engine:** V6 cylinder, triple-carburettor, 2418cc, mounted in the centre
- ★ **Bodywork:** two-door, two-seater coupé
- ★ **Top speed:** 143mph
- ★ **0-60mph acceleration time:** 6.8sec
- ★ **Maximum power:** 190bhp
- ★ **Original price:** £4500 (in 1973)

Connoisseur's choice or poverty pick? Every Stratos is a gem today yet, amazingly, Lancia could still sell you a new one in 1980. Since then, quite a few have come to a sticky end in rallying events.

> **FACT: The Stratos got its name from a glider plane whose wing shape apparently influenced the shape of the car.**

Lotus Europa

In the mid-1960s the De Tomaso Vallelunga and Lamborghini Miura had adopted the motorsport principle of putting the engine in the middle of the car and made it work on the road, but this little Lotus was the first time it had made production closer to home.

To reflect its racing influence, the Europa looked like a shrunken Le Mans racer, which was in fact no accident, since its roots were in Lotus's pitch to make an endurance racer for Ford. The Americans went with another British firm, Lola, and the result was the legendary GT40, but Lotus were clearly pleased with their own effort and used it as the basis for this. Perversely, however, whilst they were clearly proud of their first mid-engined road car, they denied even the wealthiest British dad the chance to buy it by initially selling the car only in mainland Europe.

For a dreaming dad it must have seemed like the sweet shop that would only open its doors to bloody French-exchange students. When the Europa finally went on sale in the UK you could save a few quid by buying a kit version and assembling it yourself like some sort of exotic Airfix model.

★ **Years on sale:** 1966-75
★ **Engine:** straight-four cylinder, single- or twin-carburettor, 1470-1558cc, mounted in the centre
★ **Bodywork:** two-door, two-seater coupé
★ **Top speed:** 121mph (Europa Special)
★ **0-60mph acceleration time:** 7.7sec (Europa Special)
★ **Maximum power:** 126bhp (Europa Special)
★ **Original price:** £1666 (in 1966)

Connoisseur's choice or poverty pick? Early cars, the Series I and II, had a Renault 16 engine, which is fine for reliability but a bit puny in the power stakes; the later Twin Cam and Special versions are more user-friendly.

> **FACT: The Europa was designed by a man called Ron Hickman who also came up with the earlier Lotus Elan and, somewhat improbably, that more attainable Dad-tastic staple, the Black & Decker Workmate.**

Porsche 911 Turbo

In an ordinary car you push the accelerator harder and, as you might reasonably expect, the car starts to move a little bit faster. Unfortunately, this wasn't quite the case in the wild-eyed 911 Turbo. Instead, you would press this Porsche's throttle, a small amount of acceleration might occur, there would be a pause during which you might have time to say something like, 'I thought these cars were meant to be quick' (naive) or, 'Oh dear God, here we go again, please don't let me die…' (more experienced). After which aching gap you might experience something not dissimilar to being walloped in the back by a burly man with a sledgehammer.

This was all down to the turbocharger Porsche had bolted to the 911's engine, a relatively new and novel thing back in the mid-'70s, which was tasked with forcing more air into the cylinders, to the benefit of performance. And, sure enough, the performance did benefit, it's just that the turbo's reluctance to react with anything approaching a sense of urgency meant you often had to wait a short time before the full wallop of 256 bhp arrived. Add in the handling friskiness of having the engine hanging out behind the back axle and

you can see why the 911 Turbo gained its widowmaker reputation. But perhaps that only made it more appealing to Dad as he dreamt of being the man who could finally tame this fearsome beast. If only he'd got the cash to buy one in the first place.

- ★ **Years on sale:** 1975-90
- ★ **Engine:** flat-six cylinder, triple-carburettor, 2873/3299cc, mounted at the back
- ★ **Bodywork:** two-door, 2+2 coupé, two-door, 2+2 Targa and convertible
- ★ **Top speed:** 165mph (3.3-litre)
- ★ **0-60mph acceleration time:** 5sec
- ★ **Maximum power:** 330bhp
- ★ **Original price:** £14,749 (in 1977)

Connoisseur's choice or poverty pick? The super-costly, flat-bonneted SE of 1985 was aimed at the playboy, and there was no Targa or cabriolet option until 1987. But they're all gold-plated supercars.

FACT: Despite being Porsche's top-of-the-range car, the original 911 Turbo featured an archaic four-speed gearbox simply because the modern five-speed box enjoyed by lesser models wasn't strong enough to take the mighty wallop of the turbocharged engine.

A VERY BIG HOUSE IN THE COUNTRY AND . . .

Amphicar

The desire to make a car that can also go on water has occupied the idle thoughts of engineers for years. And frankly, it's hard to understand exactly why. There can't be many people who've thought, 'I like my Volkswagen Golf but I just wish I could drive it across that lake…' Even so, the irrelevant quest to meld two different modes of transport continues, regularly throwing up another weird-looking prototype that then inevitably sinks without trace, sometimes literally.

Only one company has ever made an amphibious car that sold more than a mere handful, and that company was – the clue's in the name here – the Amphicar Corporation of Berlin. In fact, amphibious cars is all they ever did from the day the Amphicar was revealed until the fateful moment five years later when the company went out of business, but during their brief existence they sold one of the most distinctive and unique cars in the world.

The brochure cheerfully described it as a 'sports car', but with a weedy 43bhp engine from a Triumph Herald sitting at the back, the Amphicar was never going to set new performance records on the road and, though an ingenious dual gearbox allowed it to slip instantly into the drink, using the front wheels as the rudders didn't make it especially agile on water. Plus, because it was built from corrosion-prone steel it was best to avoid using it in salt water, or indeed any water at all. In other words, in its cunning attempts to fuse car and boat together, the Amphicar inevitably ended up a compromise. And did that stop Dad from wanting one? Did it heck. Because much though the Amphicar was basically irrelevant and silly, the truth is it also looked like enormous fun.

★ **Years on sale:** 1961-68
★ **Engine:** straight-four cylinder, single-carburettor, 1147cc, mounted at the back
★ **Bodywork:** two-door, four-seater convertible
★ **Top speed:** 70mph on land, 7mph (six knots) on water
★ **0-60mph acceleration time:** 42.9sec
★ **Maximum power:** 43bhp
★ **Original price:** £1275 (in 1964)

Connoisseur's choice or poverty pick? Only one model, and quite sought-after today, but you may have trouble finding one in Europe – of the 3878 made, 3046 went to the USA.

> **FACT: The Amphicar was available in four different colours, each with a suitably watery theme. They were Beach White, Regatta Red, Lagoon Blue and Fjord Green. No mention of Catastrophic Structural Rust Brown.**

Lamborghini LM002

So here's an interesting idea: a rough, tough 4x4 designed for the military which was so lumberingly massive that it made an elephant look balletic and which would enter the theatre of conflict powered by a highly strung, fuel-guzzling V12 engine from a low-slung supercar. Welcome to the insane world of the Lamborghini LM002.

Why in the name of all that's holy Lamborghini suddenly decided they should make a car for the army is anyone's guess, but at least the LM002 wasn't quite as bonkers as their first prototype, called the Cheetah, which carried a V8 engine at the back of the car where it could do unusual and terrifying things to the handling. Unsurprisingly, after testing it in California, the US Army ran a mile, preferring to give the contract for its next-generation 4x4 to a company called AM General for what eventually became the Hummer.

Unbowed, the loons at Lamborghini switched the V8 for the V12 from the Countach, moved it to the front of the car, and then smeared the interior with teak and leather, thus making the aspiring army machine into a posh SUV for civilians with more money than sense. Your dad might have aspired to own one, but frankly it would have made more sense to take you to school every day on the back of an ill-tempered rhinoceros.

* **Years on sale:** 1986-93
* **Engine:** V12 cylinder, six carburettors, 5167cc, mounted at the front
* **Bodywork:** four-door, four-seater saloon/pick-up
* **Top speed:** 117mph
* **0-60mph acceleration time:** unknown
* **Maximum power:** 444bhp
* **Original price:** not sold in the UK

Connoisseur's choice or poverty pick? You can go for the standard model, or maybe unearth one of the few equipped with Lamborghini's marine-specification V12 engine, topping out at an insane 7 litres.

> **FACT:** When American troops entered Baghdad they discovered an old LM002 belonging to Saddam Hussein's eldest son, Uday, which they decided to pack with dynamite and use to test bomb-resistant barriers. There wasn't much left of Uday's Lamborghini after that.

Land Rover 101 Forward Control

Here we have a true Dad fantasy car, largely because it wasn't even available to the public. To get his mitts on one, Dad needed to take the rather drastic step of enlisting in the armed forces, it being the British Army who had laid down the requirements for – and were the sole UK recipient of – this rugged cube of manly goodness.

Whilst lesser Land Rovers parped along with mere four-cylinder engines, the 101 rumbled into battle with the mighty V8 from a Range Rover. But it was hard to think of a greater contrast to the increasingly urbane Chelsea Tractor than this rough and tough piece of military hardware with its stripped-out interior, ability to shed bodywork until it was light enough to be lifted by a helicopter, and that truck-like cab that, unlike those on other Land Rovers, sat above the front wheels, hence the 'Forward Control' bit of its name.

To give an idea of just how functional this war-hungry hero was, Land Rover eliminated the gauges and warning lights for some of its most vital fluids by cleverly bolting their reservoir bottles straight to the dash so you could just see if they were running low. That's the kind of no-nonsense approach that made this camo-painted curio so appealing, though it wasn't until the army started selling off their

101s that Dad could dream of buying one. But whilst production ended in 1978, some of these beasts weren't demobbed until well into the '90s, suggesting that soldiering types liked their Forward Controls as much as your dad might have done.

★ **Years built:** 1975-78
★ **Engine:** V8 cylinder, single-carburettor, 3528cc, mounted at the front
★ **Bodywork:** two-door open troop carrier, radio truck or ambulance
★ **Top speed:** 75mph approx
★ **0-60mph acceleration time:** unknown
★ **Maximum power:** 135bhp
★ **Original price:** not sold to the public

Connoisseur's choice or poverty pick? Built to British Army spec, so superb for tough terrain, but any model with fixed rear bodywork will be the ultimate useful vehicle.

> **FACT: When Land Rover agreed to provide 30-odd prop cars for the 1995 movie Judge Dredd, they built the futuristic-looking vehicles on old 101 chassis.**

Range Rover

Who could have guessed that the Range Rover would one day become synonymous with bosomy, wood-and-leather-lined luxury of the highest order, because its genesis was a more basic attempt to make a car that was just slightly more comfortable than the Land Rover. And since there were camels more comfortable than a Land Rover, that wasn't hard.

The first Range Rover's interior was designed to be cleaned with a bucket of water and a mop, and even its appearance was simply a slightly smarter version of the first prototype whose body had been cobbled together just to cover the mechanical parts underneath. In other words, the Range Rover's rise to the point where it features in the back of every celebrity pap shot happened almost despite – rather than because of – Land Rover's early intentions for it.

Nonetheless, for a dad who lusted after shiny things, the Range Rover has always had appeal, not least because of its lofty and therefore rather superior driving position. For the same reason that he might fancy a penthouse apartment, Dad thought that on the day he became impossibly rich, one of the first things he wanted to do was to look down on people who weren't.

★ **Engine:** petrol V8 cylinder, single-carburettor/fuel injection, 3528-4278cc, and turbodiesel straight-four, single-carburettor /fuel injection, 2392-2495cc, mounted at the front
★ **Bodywork:** two- or four-door, five-seater estate
★ **Top speed:** 110mph (4.2-litre)
★ **0-60mph acceleration:** 10.8sec (4.2-litre)
★ **Maximum power:** 200bhp (4.2-litre)
★ **Original price:** £1998 (3.5-litre in 1970)

Connoisseur's choice or poverty pick? Hmm, anyone who's owned a V8 Range Rover will know about its prodigious thirst, but the early turbodiesel was incredibly slow, with a 92mph top speed and 0-60mph in about 17sec, despite its thrift.

> **FACT: To throw casual onlookers off the scent, Range Rover prototypes were badged 'Velar', which was both a traditional Rover subterfuge and also an easy word to make from jumbling the stick-on badging that ran across the front of a Range Rover's bonnet.**

THE CROWN PRINCE OF SOMEWHERE

Aston Martin DB5

Oh dear, it's the Aston DB5, a car that it seems to be impossible to talk about without referring to the movie career of the world's least secret secret agent. But let's be honest here, the DB5 would have been an object of lust even without the constant reference to the B-word, because it's still one of the most perfectly elegant and stylish cars ever made. Beautifully crafted too, each one of those gorgeously sculpted panels being carefully and slowly shaped by hand whilst the 4-litre straight six was intricately assembled by just one man.

The noise alone makes the DB5 a legend: carburettors sucking, exhaust barking; the sound of a different era of car design before fuel injection and catalytic converters, but with a cut-glass tone that set it apart from the run of the mill.

By modern standards the DB5 isn't actually all that fast, and round corners it would get outhandled by a basic Fiesta, but that's really not the point. Your dad wanted it because it's simply one of the coolest cars ever made. Oh, alright, and because he wanted to be James bloody Bond.

★ **Years on sale:** 1963–66
★ **Engine:** straight-six cylinder, triple-carburettor, 3995cc, mounted at the front
★ **Bodywork:** two-door, four-seater coupé; two-door, four-seater convertible
★ **Top speed:** 141mph
★ **0-60mph acceleration time:** 8.1sec
★ **Maximum power:** 282bhp
★ **Original price:** £3980 (in 1963)

Connoisseur's choice or poverty pick? Possibly beating the Bond glamour of the coupé is the DB5 convertible, and the most desirable of both would have the 314bhp Vantage engine.

> **FACT: As well as the usual acreage of leather, the DB5's interior boasted electric windows – still rare in 1963 – and a push-button radio: switch it on and the words 'Aston Martin' glowed reassuringly in red from the tuner.**

Bentley Continental S3 ▬

There's really only one word for a car like this and that word is 'magnificent'. The S3 was the last of the truly majestic Bentleys, built on a separate chassis, which meant that various coachbuilders could create their own unique bodies for it, some achingly gorgeous, others proving that money can't buy you taste (although perhaps it should be used to purchase a new pair of glasses). Later Bentley, switched to making cars with a more modern but rather less special one-piece monocoque body that ruled out lavish coachbuilding and, worse still, carried with it the whiff of – gasp! – mass production.

Thankfully, there was no such tawdry flavour to this Continental, which felt resolutely and delightfully crafted by hand to the highest possible standards, from the whispering V8 in its nose to the very tip of its aluminium tail. But it was the name that was the mark of this car. This S3 was the last in a glorious line of Bentleys using the Continental badge – after which it was 'rested' for almost 20 years – and it spoke volumes about its purpose, or at least what your dad

might imagine he would do with one. As in, 'Hello, darling, I'm in Kensington and I seem to have left my cufflinks at your place in Monte Carlo. Don't worry, I'll drive over this afternoon…'

★ **Years on sale:** 1962-65
★ **Engine:** V8 cylinder, twin-carburettor, 6230cc, mounted at the front
★ **Bodywork:** two-door, four-seater saloon; four-door, four-seater saloon; two-door, four-seater convertible
★ **Top speed:** 113mph
★ **0-60mph acceleration time:** 12sec
★ **Maximum power:** 275bhp (estimate)
★ **Original price:** up to £8000

Connoisseur's choice or poverty pick? A real choice here of opulent two-door cars and urbane Flying Spur four-door models – all panelled in aluminium to give the old girl some rapidity.

> **FACT: Right-hand drive versions of the earlier R-type Continental carried their gear lever on the right next to the driver's door. Bentley offered the option of having the lever in the middle of the car, but apparently their existing customers considered this rather vulgar.**

Bristol 411

Even by the often eccentric standards of small British car makers, Bristol Cars is a pretty strange and unusual company. Working out of a mysterious West Country factory that refuses visitors, even today their sole public outlet is a small showroom on Kensington High Street in London with an erratically illuminated sign that makes nocturnal passers-by wonder just what sort of business is done by B ISTO ARS.

It's a place that exudes a certain snootily exclusive attitude, the sort of establishment where even turning up with a suitcase full of cash and attempting to order a car might result in you being asked to leave for wearing the wrong sort of shoes.

This car, the 411, was their staple model from the late 1960s and the first half of the '70s and is arguably one of the company's prettier efforts, although only in the same way that Charlie Watts might be considered the prettiest member of the Rolling Stones. It featured the design basics that are a mark of Bristol to this day, namely a steel understructure dressed in handmade aluminium panels, a relaxed Chrysler V8 under the bonnet and all dressed up with lots of talk about 'aircraft-inspired' engineering. The 411 was a

wilfully off-beam but somehow rather wonderful car for mildly eccentric people who might consider a Rolls-Royce or Bentley just a bit too commonplace.

★ **Years on sale:** 1969-76
★ **Engine:** V8 cylinder, single-carburettor, 6277/6556cc, mounted at the front
★ **Bodywork:** two-door, four-seater saloon
★ **Top speed:** 140mph (6.6-litre)
★ **0-60mph acceleration time:** 7sec (6.2-litre)
★ **Maximum power:** 335bhp (6.2-litre)
★ **Original price:** £6997

Connoisseur's choice or poverty pick? The smaller engine is the more responsive, as the later, larger one was loaded up with power-sapping exhaust emission equipment.

> **FACT: The 411 Series 3 introduced a racy arrangement of four exhaust pipes poking from the rear. But the actual exhaust gases escaped from under the car rather than out of the pipe ends so that owners who reversed their Bristol into the garage wouldn't have to face the irritation of four sooty marks left on the back wall.**

Facel Vega HK500

The extraordinary Facel Vega was created by a patriotic Frenchman called Jean Daninos who wanted to rekindle his country's reputation for making beautifully crafted sports cars aimed at people of taste. And money. He succeeded in making his vision a reality and this, the glorious HK500, was the pinnacle of what he set out to achieve.

Whatever the French is for 'lavish', that was what Daninos had in mind for this car, from its hearty Chrysler V8 engine and weighty, handcrafted bodyshell to the finely wrought stainless-steel exterior trim and an interior so comprehensively fitted in fine materials that even the roof lining was leather.

Facel Vega cars were, unsurprisingly, meant to be exclusive, but their extravagance – and an ill-considered attempt to make engines in-house – eventually became the company's downfall, and by 1964 Facel was bankrupt. There was also the minor issue of the car's unruly road manners, that could catch unsuspecting owners out – including French literary giant Albert Camus, who perished in an HK500 smash-up.

Still, whilst the search for exclusivity became a self-fulfilling prophecy, it also made the cars even more desirable.

★ **Years on sale:** 1958-61
★ **Engine:** V8 cylinder, single-carburettor, 5907/6286cc, mounted at the front
★ **Bodywork:** two-door, four-seater coupé
★ **Top speed:** 135mph
★ **0-60mph acceleration time:** 8.4sec
★ **Maximum power:** 360bhp
★ **Original price:** £4739 (in 1960)

Connoisseur's choice or poverty pick? Exactly 164 Facel Vegas of all types were sold in the UK, and 62 are still here; the HK500 is *the* definitive model although its replacement, the Facel II, is much rarer.

FACT: Its makers claimed that the HK500 was the fastest four-seater coupé of its time. Which might explain why racing driver Stirling Moss was one of the Facel's many celebrity owners.

Iso Grifo

A background in making refrigerators, mopeds and bubble cars wouldn't necessarily be considered the best pedigree for turning your hand to sports cars, but that wasn't going to stop Iso founder, Renzo Rivolta. In 1962 he announced his modestly eponymous Rivolta GT, thus demonstrating that a) a novice company could have a crack at a prestigious coupé and b) it was a good job his surname wasn't Shufflebottom. Then, just one year later, Rivolta showed off his masterpiece, the Grifo. When it went on sale it had the looks – the work of Giorgetto Giugiaro, the Italian genius who went on to shape everything from the VW Golf to the Lotus Esprit – and, thanks to a ripplingly muscular Chevrolet V8, the performance to match.

In a time before Monte Carlo became crammed full of thick-necked Russians and libidinous racing drivers, the Grifo looked like the kind of car you wanted to use for an elegant arrival in Casino Square, though in fact the blue-collar American engine and lack of Ferrari-style pedigree didn't go down especially well amongst the old money audience this car was aimed at. Which was a shame. Especially since they'd have been quite happy to buy one of Iso's refrigerators.

- ★ **Years on sale:** 1963-74
- ★ **Engine:** V8 cylinder, single-carburettor, 5359-7443cc, mounted at the front
- ★ **Bodywork:** two-door, two-seater coupé
- ★ **Top speed:** 170mph (7-litre)
- ★ **0-60mph acceleration time:** 6.4sec (5.4-litre)
- ★ **Maximum power:** 400bhp (7-litre)
- ★ **Original price:** £5950 (5.4-litre in 1966)

Connoisseur's choice or poverty pick? In the last two years of its life, the Grifo switched to very slightly inferior Ford engines but, apart from this, they were all Chevys, and the meanest was the 7-litre unit, which Iso boasted made the Grifo a 180mph car.

> **FACT: The engineer behind the Iso Grifo, Giotto Bizzarrini, also created the legendary Ferrari 250 GTO and rather boldly claimed that the Grifo was an 'improved GTO'.**

CHAIRMEN OF THE BOARD

Bentley Mulsanne Turbo

Despite its exciting name – taken from the long straight at the Le Mans race circuit where Bentley had once given Mr Jonathan Foreigner a bloody nose – the Bentley Mulsanne was nothing more than Rolls-Royce Silver Spirit with a new radiator grille and some different badges. And whilst this was very nice, the hushed V8 engine and soft, bosomy suspension made it about as dynamically sporty as nine holes of golf.

Two years later, however, things got distinctly more interesting when the industrious chaps at the Crewe factory mated a turbocharger to that hitherto lazy 6.75-litre lump and created this remarkable gentleman thug. The factory always shied away from quoting specific power figures, preferring to say that its engine outputs were 'adequate', but with the addition of a turbo it was safe to say the Mulsanne had tipped over into 'more than adequate', so much so that its top speed had to be limited for fear that the overstressed tyres would go pop.

Yet the real joy of the Mulsanne Turbo, especially early models, which wore the same chrome-edged wheels as lesser Bentleys, was that unless you clocked the Turbo badges you would have no idea

of the hugely increased performance until this 2-ton chunk of wood-'n'-leathery splendour appeared menacingly in your mirrors. At which point you might get some sense of what it would be like to get into a high-speed chase with Buckingham Palace.

★ **Years on sale:** 1982-85
★ **Engine:** V8 cylinder, twin-carburettor, 6750cc, mounted at the centre
★ **Bodywork:** four-door, five-seater saloon
★ **Top speed:** 135mph
★ **0-60mph acceleration time:** 6.7sec
★ **Maximum power:** never disclosed
★ **Original price:** £58,613

Connoisseur's choice or poverty pick? The later Mulsanne Turbo R added fuel injection for even more stately urge but, by then, Bentley also offered the Mulsanne S which – in the face of the Turbo's horrendous running costs – is said to be the one to go for, as it's otherwise near-identical.

FACT: The Mulsanne Turbo's engine lives on to this day, in modified form, under the bonnet of the current Bentley Arnage.

Jaguar MkX

As Jaguar's 1960s flagship, the MkX was an extraordinary car, but not as extraordinary as the brochure blurb for the Americans at which it was aimed. 'The true dignity of the MkX is eloquently expressed in its interiors', it says floridly, before inexplicably claiming that 'Drama stems from regal simplicity' and that the instrument panel is 'luxuriously functional'. It's a good job the Americans don't generally use the phrase 'utter bollocks'. The really excellent part of this sales pitch, however, is when the copywriter claims that the 'theme' of the MkX is 'good taste and correctness'. Just a shame the cod-Englishness stopped before the section that read, 'Righto, I'm off to bally well have a cup of tea with some beefeaters! Toodle-pip!'

However, despite all the waffle, the MkX's interior really was a thing of wonder, not least because at least 15 trees seemed to have been involved in its construction. Whilst lesser cars might have boasted a wooden dashboard, few showed the big Jag's devotion to knotty walnut, to the extent that even the entire windscreen surround was fashioned from something that once had squirrels living in it.

The MkX's other claim to fame was as the widest saloon ever made in the UK and, whilst its ample girth appealed to Americans, it also made it slightly unwieldy on the streets of its homeland. Even so, your dad probably wanted one because all that wood and all that width really told people he'd arrived. Unless there was a narrow street on his way there, then he might not arrive at all.

★ **Years on sale:** 1961-66
★ **Engine:** straight-six cylinder, triple-carburettor, 3781/4235cc, mounted at the front
★ **Bodywork:** four-door, five-seater saloon
★ **Top speed:** 122mph (4.2-litre)
★ **0-60mph acceleration time:** 9.9sec (4.2-litre)
★ **Maximum power:** 265bhp
★ **Original price:** £2393

Connoisseur's choice or poverty pick? The larger-engined MkX, like the near-identical 420G that replaced it in 1966, has vastly better steering and gearbox than the original.

FACT: The Daimler DS420 limousine, much used by the Royal Family on State occasions and beloved of funeral directors everywhere, was based on the MkX chassis and remained in production until 1992.

Jaguar XJ12

Imagine the smallest noise in the world. A pin dropping, a mouse farting, your dad piping up when someone asks the question, Who's going to wash all these pans? All of these would have seemed cacophonous next to the noise inside a Jaguar XJ12 at idle.

Smoother than Des Lynam's single malt collection, the Jag V12 was quite simply one of the most perfectly refined engines ever made and, though it had debuted in the E-type sports car, it was in the XJ that it found its perfect home, almost inaudibly purring between the front wheels of this handsome and urbane luxury saloon whilst the driver relaxed to the point of blissful torpor in an interior furnished almost entirely in materials that once had leaves or udders. At an almost affordable price, this was the taste of true luxury. And indeed the sound. Or lack of it.

★ **Years on sale:** 1972-93
★ **Engine:** V12 cylinder, quadruple-carburettor/fuel-injected, 5343cc, mounted at the front
★ **Bodywork:** four-door, five-seater saloon
★ **Top speed:** 135mph
★ **0-60mph acceleration time:** 8.9sec
★ **Maximum power:** 299bhp (V12 HE engine)
★ **Original price:** £3726 (Series I in 1972)

Connoisseur's choice or poverty pick? The collector's peach is the Series II XJ5.3C, a beautiful two-door edition of the car of which only 1873 were sold, while the Daimler Double-Six edition of this car is scarcer still, with 399 sold.

> **FACT:** The XJ part of this saloon's name was initially just an internal codename for future models, standing for eXperimental Jaguar. Somehow the name stuck and first appeared on the XJ6 of 1968.

Mercedes-Benz 450 SEL

It might seem strange to describe a large German limousine as a dragster, but that's basically what this car was. In essence, Mercedes-Benz's crack engineering team had taken the normal, slightly ponderous S-class and, with the addition of a titanic V8 engine, transformed it into a road-ripping, tyre-shredding, wild-eyed foaming-at-the-mouth monster.

What an engine it was too, especially since with typical Benzian-over-engineering, each and every one was bench tested for almost 4 hours before being put into the car, just to make sure it was up to scratch. And, in an attempt to keep this hotrod on the road, the regular S-class suspension was replaced with hydropneumatic springs that aimed to keep the car tracking straight and true whilst maintaining a ride that was softer than a pile of kittens.

It was an extraordinary piece of kit, a sort of European take on the American muscle car, but properly and thoroughly engineered. Best of all, if you didn't want people to know about the huge power

at your disposal, Mercedes would happily delete the telltale 6.9 badge from the bootlid. Although in truth if your dad had got the money to pay for one of these upsettingly expensive rocket ships, what he'd really want is for it to be made larger. And illuminated. And with bolts of lightning coming off it.

★ **Years on sale:** 1975-80
★ **Engine:** V8 cylinder, fuel-injected, 6834cc, mounted at the front
★ **Bodywork:** four-door, five-seater saloon
★ **Top speed:** 140mph
★ **0-60mph acceleration time:** 7.3sec
★ **Maximum power:** 286bhp
★ **Original price:** £21,995

Connoisseur's choice or poverty pick? One of the greatest Mercedes-Benz saloons of all time – there's your reasoning to own one. Still, feels big and heavy by modern standards.

> **FACT:** The 450 SEL 6.9 was available with options that are commonplace today but were mind-bogglingly advanced at the time, including an in-car phone and anti-lock brakes.

Mercedes-Benz 600

It's the 1960s and you've just taken control of some previously lawless state via a bloodless coup or maybe some sort of raffle. The new presidential palace is coming along nicely but now you need an official limousine in which to cruise the streets, little flags fluttering from the bonnet as you wave benignly at the adoring crowds from the comfort of the ample back seat. Frankly, there was only one option and you're looking at it here.

The massive and imposing 600 was the limo of choice for countless heads of state, from Idi Amin to Emperor Hirohito, and for good reason. Compared to a Rolls-Royce, the big Merc was less twee and more businesslike, the kind of car that said, I love my people, but if you mess with me I will send the army to destroy your crops. It had all the luxuries a modernist premier would expect too, including a fantastic system of high-pressure hydraulics that powered the seat adjustment and – bizarrely – the windows.

In its day, this was the absolute zenith of car engineering, as well as being the ultimate in spacious, impressive official transport for

elected leaders and unelected despots the world over. Your dad quite fancied one too, perhaps as a prelude to forming his own fatherly dictatorship. Get in the Mercedes, children, we're off to annex Saffron Walden.

★ **Years on sale:** 1963-81
★ **Engine:** V8 cylinder, fuel-injected, 6332cc, mounted at the front
★ **Bodywork:** four-door, six-seater saloon; four- or six-door, eight-seater limousine
★ **Top speed:** 130mph
★ **0-60mph acceleration time:** 9.7sec
★ **Maximum power:** 250bhp
★ **Original price:** £8752 (four-door)

Connoisseur's choice or poverty pick? Every single example will have a fascinating provenance but the limos, at 20ft long, won't be too much fun for an owner-driver, no matter which plutocrat used to ride in the back.

> **FACT: It wasn't just world leaders that liked this car. John Lennon had a 600 which he later sold to George Harrison. And more recently, Jeremy Clarkson bought one.**

HE-MAN

AC Cobra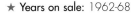

If you gave your car to the average chicken farmer, chances are they'd just get the interior all covered in eggs and hen poo. But when one-time poultry baron Carroll Shelby of Texas got hold of a small British sports car called the AC Ace, the result was rather more dramatic, if equally unsettling.

Looking for a new racing car, the failed American chick magnate asked if AC would modify their sweet, demure little roadster to take a belting Detroit V8. They agreed, and the result became the stuff of automotive legend as it began to terrify drivers on roads, on tracks, and often on its back in a ditch. Shelby claims the Cobra name came to him in a dream, but however he arrived at it, the poisonous badge seemed apt.

Shelby kept on working on his pet project, culminating in the heavily revised MkIII Cobra, its once delicate bodywork distended and swollen like a former Miss World after a heavy course of steroids,

the thundering Ford V8 now up to a massive and mighty 7 litres.

It made the Cobra more fearsome than ever, a thug of a car that needed an appetite for fighting to keep it under control. It became an icon, a car that spawned a thousand fibreglass replicas, but few could capture the brutal majesty of the legendary original. Ironically, given its history, there was one thing you couldn't be if you wanted to master a Cobra and that was . . . chicken.

★ **Years on sale:** 1962-68
★ **Engine:** V8 cylinder, single-carburettor, 4261/4727/6984/6997cc, mounted at the front
★ **Bodywork:** two-door, two-seater roadster
★ **Top speed:** 165mph (Cobra 427)
★ **0-60mph acceleration time:** 4sec (Cobra 427 S/C)
★ **Maximum power:** 425bhp (Cobra 427)
★ **Original price:** £2454 (in 1963)

Connoisseur's choice or poverty pick? Some estimates put the total of Cobra replicas at 100,000. Hardly surprising when 979 real ones were made. The purity of the earlier 289 makes it the collector's fave, although replica makers mostly mimic the 427.

> **FACT:** Having announced the Cobra to the world, Shelby had trouble getting production started. But to give the impression that assembly was in full swing, every time the one and only prototype was lent to a car magazine it was resprayed a different colour.

Austin-Healey 3000

This car was often referred to as the 'Big Healey' even though by modern standards it's positively titchy, coming in at about the same length as a Renault Clio and well over a foot narrower to boot. But actually, the 'Big' name wasn't really about mere physical dimensions. It was more about the hearty engine under the bonnet – a fruity 2.9-litre straight six snorting through SU carbs – and frankly about the car as a whole. Because though it doesn't seem literally 'big', there was something very strapping and man-size about the 3000.

It was sturdy and heavy, the kind of car that would be driven not by blokes but by chaps. If you didn't own at least one thing made of tweed and enjoy a good pint of foaming brown ale with bits of soil floating in it, maybe you just weren't a Big Healey sort of fellow.

The 3000 even came with its own widowmaker tale which suggested that, because the steering column started perilously close to the front of the car, in an accident the entire wheel would be slammed into your chest with potentially gruesome consequences.

But that didn't stop your dad from wanting a Big Healey, nor indeed did it prevent people from buying them. Well really, if it worried you that much what were you? A cissy?

★ **Years on sale:** 1959-67
★ **Engine:** straight-six cylinder, twin-carburettor, 2912cc, mounted at the front
★ **Bodywork:** two-door, two- or 2+2-seater roadster
★ **Top speed:** 121mph (MkIII)
★ **0-60mph acceleration time:** 9.8sec (MkIII)
★ **Maximum power:** 148bhp (MkIII)
★ **Original price:** £1168

Connoisseur's choice or poverty pick? The MkIII is certainly the best and beefiest Big Healey, with a better interior, and 2+2 seating, which should delight your children.

> **FACT: Towards the end of the 3000's life, the factory literally split one in half, widened it by six inches, and fitted a new 4-litre engine in the hope that it would give the car a new lease of life. Sadly, their paymasters at BMC said no and the old beast died soon afterwards.**

Jaguar XKSS

The famous Jaguar D-type racing car, all glinting latent aggression and sharky rear fin, was a hero on the racetrack, winning the Le Mans 24 Hours race in 1954, '55 and '56. Over in the United States it also grabbed the top spot in the 1955 Sebring 12 Hours race too, but Jaguar felt its racing opportunities were limited on that side of the Atlantic because the pesky Sports Car Club of America wouldn't let the D-type race in its production sports car class. Upper lips duly stiffened, Jaguar set about bally well sorting that with a more road-friendly D-type that would appease those impudent Yanks. And this was the result. Brutal, beautiful, sought-after: the Jaguar XKSS.

To create their race hero in a morning suit, Jaguar took a D-type – customer demand had dropped off and they had plenty sitting idle at the factory – gave it two seats, lopped off the fin and added a veneer of civilisation with stuff like bumpers and that visor-ish windscreen. The end result was glorious and Jag should have had no trouble selling the 50 cars they intended to make. Except that on 12 February 1957 a fire gutted Jaguar's Coventry plant, destroying nine half-built XKSSs and all the tooling needed to complete them.

That was it for this gentrified Le Mans winner with a body like a

sock full of squash balls. Just 16 cars made it out of the factory; after the fire only two more were created from spare D-types before Jaguar called it a day. In doing so, one of the most lusted-after cars ever built became even more desirable because of its rarity.

★ **Years on sale:** 1957
★ **Engine:** straight-six cylinder, triple-carburettor, 3442cc, mounted at the front
★ **Bodywork:** two-door, two-seater roadster
★ **Top speed:** 140mph
★ **0-60mph acceleration time:** 5.5sec
★ **Maximum power:** 250bhp
★ **Original price:** £2464

Connoisseur's choice or poverty pick? Even of the 16 XKSSs made, several have been highly modified into hybrid-D-types, making the task of finding an original specimen near-impossible. Fortunately, Lynx Motors builds a stunning replica, for £200,000!

> **FACT: Of the handful of XKSSs made, most went to the USA, including one for a well-known car enthusiast called Steve McQueen.**

Lotus 7

Your dad could do nothing more than dream about a lot of the cars in this book because they were expensive, rare or both. But here's a car that he probably couldn't have, not because of its huge price tag or rooster's toothbrush rarity, but because you built it yourself. Maybe your dad was a practical chap and quite useful with a set of spanners, but how many mums would actually let him disappear into the garage for weeks on end, especially when the result would be a frivolous two-seater sports car?

The 7 came into being in the late '50s, at a time when new car prices were elevated by stinging purchase tax. But kit cars were exempt from this, which is why most 7 buyers took delivery of a series of boxes and assembled it themselves, as if they were tackling grown-up Meccano. But this wasn't simply a way to get cheap transport, because the 7 was a fine car in its own right, shot through with Lotus's obsessive quest for simplicity and lightness.

For sheer thrills, it was a belter even though Lotus boss Colin Chapman didn't seem that fond of it. For him this was just a stopgap, a cunning scheme to fund production of his real baby, a more complex coupé called the Elite. When the 7 was announced at the 1957 Earls Court Motor Show, Chapman didn't even bother to display an actual car, just a sad stack of brochures. Yet, despite sounding like the runt of the litter, the 7 was a success for Lotus and, when Chapman wanted to push upmarket into fully built cars, he sold the rights to a company called Caterham, which continues to thrive making 7s to this day. As Dad might wistfully point out, you can still have them in kit form too.

★ **Years on sale:** 1957-73
★ **Engine:** straight-four cylinder, single- or twin-carburettor, 948-1599cc, mounted at the front
★ **Bodywork:** doorless two-seater roadster
★ **Top speed:** 110mph (Series III Super Sprint)
★ **0-60mph acceleration time:** 7.1sec (MkIII)
★ **Maximum power:** 125bhp (Series III Super Sprint)
★ **Original price:** £1036 (£536 in kit form)

Connoisseur's choice or poverty pick? The 7 came back to life after 1973 thanks to Caterham. The first thing they did was axe the Series IV and return to the Series III. So the unloved IV offers good value.

> **FACT: The tax-dodging kit-car rules bizarrely stated that the box of bits could not contain instructions. So Lotus included some pages from a magazine, which helpfully explained how to dismantle a fully built 7. All you had to do was follow the article in reverse.**

Morgan Plus 8

Morgan isn't a company to make radical changes for the sake of it. They introduced their first four-wheeled car in 1936, and that basic design with its wooden frame and Edwardian suspension (no, really, the front axle had its roots in 1909) remained the same thereafter. That is until the late '60s when the gasping, four-cylinder Triumph motor they used at the time was axed. Bit of a bally nuisance and all that. Except that, as luck would have it, Rover had recently approached Morgan with the suggestion of a sports car tie-up and, whilst this had come to nothing, it had made the chaps at the little factory in Worcestershire aware of Rover's new V8. By golly, if you stuck it in something as light as a Morgan, that would blow the crumbs out of your 'tache.

Rover's bosses were sceptical, at least until they took a spin in Morgan's V8 prototype, after which the deal was done. At a stroke that most cautious of car makers had transformed their enduring sports car from tweedy sluggard into serious road rocket. You'd have to wait anything up to ten years between ordering your Plus 8 and actually getting it. Which meant Dad could idly imagine buying one on the sly, timed to turn up just after the kids left home.

★ **Years on sale:** 1968-2004
★ **Engine:** V8 cylinder, twin-carburettor/ fuel-injected, 3528/3946cc, mounted at the front
★ **Bodywork:** two-door, two-seater roadster
★ **Top speed:** 124mph (3.5-litre twin-carburettor)
★ **0-60mph acceleration time:** 5.6sec (3.5-litre fuel-injected)
★ **Maximum power:** 190bhp (3.9-litre)
★ **Original price:** £1478

Connoisseur's choice or poverty pick? Choose one built after 1986 because their ash frames were treated with Cuprinol wood preservative, and so last much longer...

FACT: Morgan's massive waiting list was famously highlighted by the 1990 BBC programme Troubleshooter, in which Sir John Harvey-Jones told the company to modernise or go under. They politely ignored much of his advice but did reorganise; today, the waiting list is down to a year.

Sunbeam Tiger

In the 1950s and '60s, British sports cars were a big hit in the United States and, keen to steal a slice of the action from rivals like MG, the Rootes Group embarked on a serious attempt to win over the Americans with a smart-looking soft top of their own. The result was the Sunbeam Alpine and, with its cute looks and neat folding roof, it had everything the American roadster fan could want. Well, almost everything. The only snag was performance, or rather lack of it, because to American minds the Alpine's weedy four-cylinder engine couldn't pull a drifter off your sister.

At the suggestion of their West Coast representative, Rootes agreed to find an engine with a bit more hair on its chest, and eventually alighted on a 4.2-litre V8 from Ford in Detroit. The job of fitting this engine into the first prototype was given to a man who knew a thing or two about shoehorning American muscle into lightweight British roadsters, AC Cobra creator Carroll Shelby; once Rootes bosses were satisfied that this Anglo-American union would work, they contracted Jensen to build the car for them. Job's a good 'un.

Sadly, the Tiger's life was a short one. By 1967 Rootes had been bought by American giant Chrysler, who didn't take kindly to the idea of selling a car powered by one of their rival's engines, and the Tiger was killed off. Plans were drawn up for a new, larger replacement car with a V8 from Chrysler, but there was no money in the pot to make it and one of the most excellent names in car history was laid to rest for good. Grrrr.

- ★ **Years on sale:** 1964-68
- ★ **Engine:** V8 cylinder, single-carburettor, 4260/4727cc, mounted at the front
- ★ **Bodywork:** two-door, two-seater roadster
- ★ **Top speed:** 125mph (Tiger II)
- ★ **0-60mph acceleration time:** 7.5sec (Tiger II)
- ★ **Maximum power:** 200bhp (Tiger II)
- ★ **Original price:** £1446

Connoisseur's choice or poverty pick? The Tiger II is the better car but you're very unlikely to find one as almost all of the 571 built were sold in the USA. Tigers Is, with 6495 built, are still much sought-after.

> **FACT:** To get the Ford V8 into the engine bay, parts of the basic Alpine's inner bodywork had to be bent out of the way. When Chrysler took over the company they tried to install their own V8 but just couldn't hammer away enough metal to make it fit.

TVR 350i

The TVR 350i was a great British bruiser in the best tradition of the AC Cobra and Sunbeam Tiger, using the same trick of taking a lightweight British roadster and replacing its uninspiring engine with a whacking great American V8. Except in the TVR's case, the engine wasn't strictly from the United States, and deliberately so. Sure, the Rover V8 had its roots in Detroit, being originally designed by Buick, but it had been modified by the British and was built in a UK factory.

This, as it turned out, was a crucial factor when TVR went looking for a new engine to power its wedgy Tasmin range. Until that point these cars had run Ford V6 engines, but this wasn't going down well in one of their largest export markets, Saudi Arabia, where the delicate political climate of the day meant anything perceived as American (even though this particular Ford engine came from Germany) was seen as undesirable. The Rover engine solved that problem nicely, and as an added bonus it gave the car mighty performance and an exhaust note that sounded like the God of Thunder burping up fireworks.

★ **Years on sale:** 1984-89
★ **Engine:** V8 cylinder, fuel-injected, 3528cc, mounted at the front
★ **Bodywork:** two-door, two-seater roadster
★ **Top speed:** 136mph
★ **0-60mph acceleration time:** 6.6sec
★ **Maximum power:** 190bhp
★ **Original price:** £14,800

Connoisseur's choice or poverty pick? The wedge-shaped TVRs have been out of fashion for a long time, but offer tremendous thrills-per-pound. This 3.5-litre car is possibly the simplest and most enjoyable, more rapid than the older Ford V6-powered models and more robust than the later 3.9-, 4.0- and 4.2-litre TVRs.

> **FACT: The 350 is a bizarre grab-bag of bits from other cars, including Ford Granada suspension parts, Austin Princess front brakes, Ford Fiesta door locks and – on later cars – rear lights from the rather obscure Renault Fuego.**

BEAUTIFUL BEASTS

Alfa Romeo Tipo 33 Stradale

Plenty of cars might quite rightly be described as 'beautiful', and the Alfa Tipo 33 Stradale is without doubt one of them, but there's something more to it than that. Look at those buxom wheel arches, the saucily curvaceous hips, the pert bottom. This car wasn't just beautiful; it looked utterly, utterly filthy. Behind its dirty, come-hither looks there were real brains too, because this Alfa offered sophistication almost unheard of in road cars at the time, including double wishbone suspension, ventilated disc brakes, a six-speed gearbox and a V8 engine that revved to 10,000 rpm.

Such extraordinary technology was made possible because, behind the sexy bodywork, the Stradale was really an exotic racing car, lightly tamed for the road. As a result of this highly strung nature – and a painfully high price tag – only a handful of people actually went ahead and bought one. Everyone else was just content to gawp at it, secretly knowing that, even if they could get close, it would probably break them. But somehow that just made it even more attractive.

★ **Years on sale:** 1967-71
★ **Engine:** V8 cylinder, fuel-injected, 1995cc, mounted in the centre
★ **Bodywork:** two-door, two-seater coupé
★ **Top speed:** 160mph
★ **0-60mph acceleration time:** 5.5sec
★ **Maximum power:** 230bhp
★ **Original price:** not sold in the UK

Connoisseur's choice or poverty pick? An almost mythical Alfa Romeo but, assuming you can afford the $1m value each one has today, can you then stretch to the giant maintenance, service and tuning costs of driving it a few times each summer?

> **FACT:** Although this car's name sounds quite groovy to English ears, it's probably not quite so alluring to Italians for whom it's simply the 'Type 33 Street'.

Aston Martin DB4 Zagato

The Aston Martin DB4 was not what you'd ever call an ugly car. In fact, you'd find less attractive things attached to Hugh Hefner. And yet in 1960 Italian design house Zagato managed to improve on the fabulous original with this frankly staggering piece of automotive sculpture.

Given its supermodel looks, you might have expected the DB4 Zagato to be simply some preening street machine, but for Aston Martin its primary purpose was to go racing, being even lighter than the short wheelbase DB4 GT upon which it was based. Of course, lucky customers with enough cash could have one of their own for the road, but demand wasn't massive and – though 25 cars were planned – in the end just 19 originals rumbled out of Zagato's workshops, each handcrafted to the buyer's exact specifications. One customer, for example, was worried that the lightweight panels would pick up dings and asked for his entire car

to be made of slightly thicker-gauge aluminium, which the factory was happy to do. It was the kind of wallet-ravaging personal service that your dad was unlikely to get with his Ford Cortina.

★ **Years on sale:** 1960-63
★ **Engine:** straight-six cylinder, triple-carburettor, 3670cc, mounted at the front
★ **Bodywork:** two-door, two-seater coupé
★ **Top speed:** 160mph
★ **0-60mph acceleration time:** 8.5sec
★ **Maximum power:** 314bhp
★ **Original price:** £3750

Connoisseur's choice or poverty pick? There were 19 of these originally, but market demand persuaded Aston Martin and Zagato to make four more in 1991, which are known as the 'Sanction II' cars; they're authentic, but not quite the real deal.

FACT: The DB4 Zagato was designed by a man called Ercole Spada, who in later years also created the rather less beautiful Fiat Tipo, Alfa Romeo 155 and Nissan Terrano.

Ferrari 250 GTO

Looking at it dispassionately, it's hard to see why this has become arguably the most famous and undoubtedly the most valuable Ferrari ever made. Truth be told, it was simply an evolution of the earlier 250 GT short wheelbase and a car that suffered a slightly tortured gestation: Enzo Ferrari fell out with its designers, and the first prototype, having been shown off to the press, proved itself to be unstable during tests until they hastily bolted that little ducktail spoiler to the back.

But if you're going to be dispassionate about things, you might also say that Frank Sinatra's singing sometimes sounded a bit flat and that the Mona Lisa should bloody well cheer up. Because this car – officially known as the 250 GT Comp/62; the GTO bit crept in later – was more than the sum of its parts. It was in fact a pure embodiment of all that is good and special about Ferrari.

And of course it was beautiful, with that long, snake-like nose that appeared to be taking the squat, muscular rear and dragging it forwards. It was no mere beauty queen either, enjoying a convincing racing career including victories at the Le Mans 24 Hours and the Sebring 12 Hours races. Add rarity into the mix and you begin to

understand why, if one of the 36 made came up for sale, you'd better have about eleventy squillion quid in the bank to join the bidding. All told, the GTO is quite simply the very essence of Ferrari.

★ **Years on sale:** 1962-64
★ **Engine:** V12 cylinder, six carburettors, 2953cc, mounted at the front
★ **Bodywork:** two-door, two-seater coupé
★ **Top speed:** 157mph
★ **0-60mph acceleration time:** 6.1sec
★ **Maximum power:** 300bhp
★ **Original price:** £14,800

Connoisseur's choice or poverty pick? 'Poverty' and 'GTO' are rarely uttered in the same breath. There were only 36 GTOs, and the last one to sell at auction in 1991 in the USA made $5.5m, while another is thought to have changed hands privately in Japan for $15m. Yeah, but are their owners really happy? Really?

FACT: The 250 GTO was the first Ferrari with a metal, 'open gate' gearchange, a feature which remains on their cars to this day.

Maserati Ghibli

It's 1969 and for some reason you've agreed to give Marianne Faithfull a lift from London to Geneva to pick up some cheese or something. Well, it might have happened. Anyway, if it did, this is exactly the sort of car you'd want to be in.

A long and languid-looking grand tourer with a V8 under its extraordinarily low bonnet, a laid-back interior trimmed in fine, supple leather and two improbably long exhaust pipes poking brazenly from under the tail to give that satisfying sense of, Yes, actually mine really is bigger than yours.

The Ghibli seemed to encapsulate a mythical time when Europe was positively crawling with impossibly cool playboys frittering away their days powering around the continent in their decadent grand touring cars. Powering at some speed too, especially if Count Di Molto Cashi had chosen the later Ghibli SS, its engine plumped up from 4.7 to 4.9 litres.

And to make sure he wouldn't have to stop too often on his

random transcontinental dash, Maserati thoughtfully gave the Ghibli range-boosting twin fuel tanks, proving that they really knew a thing or two about how this car was going to be used. Although maybe not about the specific Marianne cheese mission. Which, on reflection, probably never happened. Oh well.

★ **Years on sale:** 1967-73
★ **Engine:** V8 cylinder, quadruple-carburettor, 4719/4930cc, mounted at the front
★ **Bodywork:** two-door, two-seater coupé; two-door, two-seater roadster
★ **Top speed:** 165mph (4.9-litre SS)
★ **0-60mph acceleration time:** 7sec (4.9-litre SS)
★ **Maximum power:** 335bhp
★ **Original price:** £10,180

Connoisseur's choice or poverty pick? A stunning car in every way, you'd be fortunate and loaded to own an SS Spider, which is the rarest example, only a little less so to possess the bottom-of-the-barrel (remember, it's all relative…) 4.7 coupé.

> **FACT:** The Ghibli coupé may have been beautiful but it was also quite literally a pain in the neck, being just 46 inches high, and therefore pretty uncomfortable for anyone tall who quaintly insisted on bringing their head with them.

MID-ENGINED CRISIS

BMW M1

Quite an unusual car this, being a mid-engined coupé from a company that was most famous for upright saloons. BMW realised that they might be out of their depth with their brave new break from the norm and so very sensibly got in some hired help. Persuading design maestro Giorgetto Giugiaro to style it? Great idea. Asking a load of top-notch suppliers, such as Recaro seats, to supply the parts for the car? Again, a great idea. And commissioning supercar experts Lamborghini to develop and build the whole thing? Ah, actually that wasn't a great idea at all.

You see, the Italians took the money BMW gave them and foolishly blew a big chunk of it on their own Cheetah 4x4 project, after which they promptly went bust. The Germans took matters into their own hands, dispatched trucks across the Alps to seize the Lamborghini-built M1 prototypes from under the Italian receiver's nose and finished the job themselves. They did rather nicely too, as the M1 became famed as one mid-engined car that was well made and civilised enough to use like a normal car. Assuming, that is, you could afford one, or indeed find one – because M1s were rare. Just over 450 were made, and many were smashed up when BMW, having failed to enter it in sports-car racing, created the one-make Procar series in which F1 drivers competed in track-spec M1s. It was quite a spectacle.

★ **Years on sale:** 1979-80
★ **Engine:** straight-six cylinder, fuel-injected, 3453cc, mounted in the centre
★ **Bodywork:** two-door, two-seater coupé
★ **Top speed:** 162mph
★ **0-60mph acceleration time:** 5.5sec
★ **Maximum power:** 277bhp
★ **Original price:** £37,570

Connoisseur's choice or poverty pick? Less than 500 exist, and this remains BMW's only mid-engined road car, and an unknown quantity except to those in 'the know'. You won't find one in *Auto Trader*...

> **FACT: Italdesign has designed dozens of cars we know and love, but the M1 is the only car Giugiaro's company was also involved in manufacturing, building the bodies at its own factory before shipping them to Germany for final assembly.**

DE TOMASO *"Pantera L."*

De Tomaso Pantera

During the 1960s, Ford in America had been ruefully eyeing the success of the Chevrolet Corvette and decided that it too should have a sexy sports car at the top of its range. In fact, they would go one better than those varmints at Chevy by making their flagship mid-engined, oh yes, and they would achieve this with a little help from a proper, bona fide Italian sports-car maker.

Unfortunately, Ferrari and Ford had become fierce rivals on the racetrack, so it wouldn't be them, and Lamborghini was probably bankrupt again that week, so Ford turned to their chums at De Tomaso who they'd been supplying with engines for some time. The Italian company had a perfect mid-engined design on the drawing board and rushed it through so that Ford could start selling the car in America. There's a flaw in that last sentence. Yes, it's the word 'rushed'.

Turns out, even by the less than impeccable standards of the '70s, the Pantera was pretty flaky, and after just three years Ford gave up on its attempts to sell a Corvette rival. De Tomaso were not beaten, however, and carried on making the Pantera, right up until 1991. Like the rock band of the same name, it wasn't subtle nor especially sophisticated, but it lasted a surprisingly long time – so someone must have liked it.

★ **Years on sale:** 1970-93
★ **Engine:** V8 cylinder, single-carburettor, 5763cc, mounted in the centre
★ **Bodywork:** two-door, two-seater coupé
★ **Top speed:** 160mph (GTS)
★ **0-60mph acceleration time:** 5.5sec (GTS)
★ **Maximum power:** 350bhp (GTS)
★ **Original price:** £6696

Connoisseur's choice or poverty pick? Never a very reliable supercar, and early ones were plagued by rust. Most went to the USA but a few were sold across Europe, and the less highly strung Pantera L (for luxury) probably makes the best road car today. You'll have your work cut out keeping a Pantera on song.

> **FACT: Elvis famously grew impatient with his Pantera when it refused to start, pulled out a handgun and shot it several times. You can still see his yellow car, complete with ballistics damage in the floor and steering wheel, at a car museum in Los Angeles.**

Ferrari Dino 246 GT

If you wanted to give a masterclass in how the perfect mid-engined sports car should look, there wouldn't be a better starting point than this. The Dino is the most exquisitely proportioned, most delicately detailed example of the art the world has ever seen, and its influence lived on far longer than the car itself.

Look at the original Lotus Elise, for example, and you won't be surprised to learn that the bloke who designed it had a Dino in his garage at home. But, though it ranks as one of the prettiest Ferraris ever made, the company never put their own name to it. Its little V6 engine, initially just 2 litres rising to 2.4 in the 246 version, was a contrast to the thumping V12s that the company had made its road-car trademark and, to avoid diluting the stout bloodline, this car was badged simply as 'Dino', a tribute to Enzo Ferrari's beloved son who had died some 11 years earlier and who, the factory liked to claim, had designed the basics for the race-car engine that was adapted to power it.

So keen were Ferrari to distance this car from its bigger brothers that their famous prancing horse logo appears only on the chassis plate, hidden well inside the

engine bay. Every other badge simply read 'Dino'. Yet despite this, the little GT was so beautiful, so spirited and became so legendary that, whatever the badges might have said, it had the soul of a real Ferrari.

* ★ **Years on sale:** 1969-73
* ★ **Engine:** V6 cylinder, triple-carburettor, 2418cc, mounted in the centre
* ★ **Bodywork:** two-door, two-seater coupé
* ★ **Top speed:** 148mph
* ★ **0-60mph acceleration time:** 7.1sec
* ★ **Maximum power:** 195bhp
* ★ **Original price:** £5486

Connoisseur's choice or poverty pick? There is a poor relation to the 246 GT and it's the short-lived 206 GT, with a 2-litre engine, made between 1967 and '69. It has rarity and curiosity values on its side, but the 246 is a far better bet.

> **FACT: Looking after your Dino would have been a bit of a pain back in 1971. It needed servicing and greasing every 3,000 miles and there were only seven Ferrari dealers in the UK. Still, at least the fusebox was labelled in three languages (including English).**

Lotus Esprit

If you were a dreaming dad or a child of a certain era, forget your Ferraris and Lamborghinis, this is how a supercar should look. The Esprit wasn't always the fastest or indeed the best piece of exotica on the block but it had all the low-slung, impossibly wedge-shaped drama you'd ever want, and that was what really mattered, especially if you couldn't actually afford one. Chalk up yet another superb bit of work to Italian car sketchist par excellence, Giorgetto Giugiaro.

The very first Esprits are particularly pure and clean looking, before the extra scoops and bigger lights of later models started to bulk out the shape. However, the real daddy of Esprits came in 1980, with the grunty Turbo version which, with its bigger spoilers, cross spoke alloys and large stickers on the side, could barely have been more fantastically '80s if the interior had been equipped with two crates of Quatro and both members of Yazoo.

Unsurprisingly, given its high-drama looks, the Esprit enjoyed quite an onscreen career, starring in two Bond movies, plus *Pretty Woman*, *Basic Instinct* – and of course that pinnacle of moving image glamour and excitement, the title sequence to Noel Edmonds' *Late Late Breakfast Show*.

★ **Years on sale:** 1976-2004
★ **Engine:** straight-four cylinder, twin-carburettor/fuel-injected, 1973-2174cc and V8 cylinder, fuel-injected, 3506cc, mounted in the centre
★ **Bodywork:** two-door, two-seater coupé
★ **Top speed:** 175mph (V8)
★ **0-60mph acceleration time:** 4.8sec (V8)
★ **Maximum power:** 350bhp (V8 Sport 350)
★ **Original price:** £5729

Connoisseur's choice or poverty pick? Of the original-style cars, the Esprit S3 without turbo is probably the best all-rounder (the Turbo is considerably faster), while the top dog of the post-1988 restyle models is the V8 SE, although there's a plethora of specialised variants too.

> **FACT: Designer Giorgetto Giugiaro wanted Lotus to call this car 'Kiwi'. Thankfully, the company had a tradition of model names starting with 'E', which maybe made it easier for them to tell him to sod off.**

Maserati Bora

When, in the late 1960s, Maserati decided to follow the growing trend for mid-engined road cars, not everyone at the company was convinced. Specifically, their chief test driver, who thought there was nothing wrong with the engine being at the front of the car, as it was in all their other models. As a result, he grumpily set about trying to find fault with the Bora and tried to prove that it was no better than the front-engined cars he loved so dearly. This, as it turns out, might have been a good thing, because his efforts to pick holes in every aspect of the car just made the engineers work harder to fix them, and the end result was a masterpiece.

In particular, whilst other mid-engined cars were rough and raucous like the racers from which they took inspiration, the Bora never lost sight of Maserati's reputation for building fabulous and comfortable grand touring machines. To this end, the engine compartment was stuffed with soundproofing, there was a reasonably sized boot in the front, and the interior featured superbly louche one-piece seats that were fixed to the floor whilst the wheel and pedals moved to suit your driving position. They even put little rubber strips down the side to protect your precious

Bora against oiks in car parks dinking its panels with their doors. This sort of thoughtfulness made the Bora an altogether more civilised way to enjoy a mid-engined car. As even the ill-tempered test driver would have to agree.

★ **Years on sale:** 1972-83
★ **Engine:** V6 cylinder, fuel-injected, 1999/2965cc, mounted in the centre
★ **Bodywork:** two-door, two-seater coupé
★ **Top speed:** 153mph (3-litre SS)
★ **0-60mph acceleration time:** 7.8sec (3-litre SS)
★ **Maximum power:** 220bhp (3-litre SS)
★ **Original price:** £7966

Connoisseur's choice or poverty pick? You won't find a 2-litre outside Italy, where it was sold exclusively to duck under a punishing tax band for cars with bigger engines, but you wouldn't want anything but the bigger engine anyway.

> **FACT: Maserati named its cars after winds, in this case one that sweeps in from the Adriatic. Unfortunately, VW also likes a wind-based name and in 1998 adopted the Bora badge for an unglamorous saloon version of the Golf.**

Renault 5 Turbo

Wouldn't you have loved to have been in the mid-'70s meeting when they decided to do this car? Right, they would have said (but in French, probably). We need a new world rally car: which of our models shall we use? Someone would have suggested the Renault 5 and everyone would have snorted and shrugged at the notion of sending granny's front-wheel drive runabout into battle on the dirt tracks of the world. No, no, wait, this chap would have pleaded. Why don't we make it mid-engined…?

Obviously this is a complicated and preposterous idea, but somehow Renault said yes and this was the result. Looks – vaguely – like a Renault 5, but with a manic turbocharged engine slap, bang, right where the back seats would normally be. A bonkers idea then, but actually quite a good one too, because the little 5 proved to be a popular rally weapon for many years and, by the middle of the 1980s, Peugeot, Lancia and Austin Rover were all fielding their own mid-engined mud monsters very loosely based on existing hatchbacks.

Of course, what your dad wanted was the road-car version, if only so he could pull up alongside Porsches at the lights, allow them to assume he was driving a shopping car with a bad bodykit, and then pulverise them off the line.

* ★ **Years on sale:** 1980-86
* ★ **Engine:** straight-four cylinder, fuel-injected, 1397cc, mounted in the centre
* ★ **Bodywork:** three-door, two-seater hatchback
* ★ **Top speed:** 126mph
* ★ **0-60mph acceleration time:** 7.3sec
* ★ **Maximum power:** 160bhp
* ★ **Original price:** not sold in the UK

Connoisseur's choice or poverty pick? Well, if you like the look of the 5 Turbo but can't face the raw driving experience, you could always go for a normal Renault 5 Gordini Turbo with an engine in the front and folding seats in the back.

> **FACT: The Renault 5 Turbo was built on a dedicated production line at the Alpine factory in sunny Dieppe. The first one screeched off the end of it on 20 May 1980; 802 cars and three years later, it was all over, but only after the car won the 1981 Monte Carlo Rally.**

JET SET

Audi Quattro

Four-wheel drive sports cars had never really worked until the Audi Quattro came along. Sure, Jensen had a go with their FF coupé in the '60s, but otherwise the idea that four-wheel drive was good seemed stuck on the farm. Even the Quattro itself had its roots in more agricultural machinery, a VW 4x4 called the Iltis designed for the German Army. But Audi's boffins saw potential in its 4WD system and secretly grafted it under an anonymous 80 saloon before inviting their VW bosses to try the car on the slippery roads of the Austrian Alps. They were impressed and approved it for production, possibly by barking the words 'Fire up the Quattro!' But in German.

Some of the early advertising for the car ran with the line 'Don't try to catch a Quattro in the snow', as if they couldn't quite get away from its Land Rover-ish roots, but the truth was that even on a crisp, dry day the Quattro clung to the road like day-old Weetabix to a bowl. That four-wheel drive grip also gave it an epic rallying career that peaked with the snorting Quattro Sport, a rare special featuring a shorter wheelbase for better agility and – somewhat bizarrely – the gawky, more upright windscreen from the Audi 80 saloon, apparently for better visibility and so drivers had more room for their crash-helmeted heads.

Audi's rallying rivals came up with their own four-wheel-drive cars, but nothing could take away from the fact that the Quattro was truly an original.

★ **Years on sale:** 1980-89
★ **Engine:** straight-five cylinder, fuel-injected, 2144/2226cc, mounted at the front
★ **Bodywork:** two-door, four-seater coupé
★ **Top speed:** 135mph (2.2-litre)
★ **0-60mph acceleration time:** 6.3sec (2.2-litre)
★ **Maximum power:** 200bhp
★ **Original price:** £14,500

Connoisseur's choice or poverty pick? Early Quattros were left-hand drive only and did not feature anti-lock brakes, and are maybe the ones to avoid for maximum enjoyment. A quintessential 1980s classic.

> *FACT: The Quattro was equipped with a centre differential to stop the drivetrain tangling itself in knots at low speed because one of Audi's senior engineers lent the prototype to his wife and she pointed out that it was hard to park.*

BMW 6-Series

Although there are lots of animals that might inspire a car designer, there can't be many better than the shark. And BMW clearly agreed when they came up with this: the low, sinister and distinctly aquatic 6-series. It was the kind of car that you might imagine would get its kicks from repeatedly attacking Roy Scheider. Yet, despite that threatening and possibly leg-severing appearance, this car was actually all about safety.

BMW had made big coupés before, but when the Americans announced new and severe crash test regulations in the 1970s, their delicate pillarless side windows weren't strong enough to withstand whatever the regulators were planning to throw at them. Unbowed, the Germans came up with this: a brand-new and rather cool coupé, based on the 5-series saloon but with a body that could withstand even the toughest impact testing. The 6-series team were very proud of how tough their new coupé was, even going so far as to christen its series of crumple zones and reinforcements with the slightly overdramatic title 'BMW Life Saving System'.

It was all very reassuring, as was the introduction of a vaguely high-tech 'check panel' grid of warning lights which looked like a '70s computer game and warned you if vital fluid levels were low,

rear light bulbs were blown or if Robert Shaw was trying to harpoon you again. Oh, alright, maybe not that last one.

★ **Years on sale:** 1976-89
★ **Engine:** straight-six cylinder, single-carburettor/fuel-injected, 2788-3453cc, mounted in the centre
★ **Bodywork:** two-door, four-seater coupé
★ **Top speed:** 150mph (M635CSi)
★ **0-60mph acceleration time:** 6sec (M635CSi)
★ **Maximum power:** 286bhp (M635CSi)
★ **Original price:** £13,980 (630CS)

Connoisseur's choice or poverty pick? The M635CSi is the ultimate version, with its special body kits, wheels and interior, and is acknowledged as the finest of a wide bunch. Most of us, though, would be perfectly chuffed to own a standard 635CSi.

> **FACT:** Although the shark-like nose is one of the 6-series' most distinctive features, designer Paul Bracq initially sketched out some alternatives that featured a radically backwards-slanted grille and even pop-up headlights.

Mercedes 500SEC

For a daydreaming dad, the appeal of this massive Merc might have been that it had two proper seats in the back. It was still an elegant coupé, but if he could actually afford one it would have seemed almost rational, since it could accommodate the kids too. Yet despite this veneer of practicality, there was something fantastically decadent and selfish about shunning a proper saloon in favour of a big car with two doors, like booking yourself into first class on a flight and making the family travel economy.

But there was nothing economy about the way the SEC was put together. It took almost ten years to develop and this engineering rigour showed itself in the smoothness of the V8 engine, the meaty weight of the doors and the sturdy click of the switches. The attention to detail was sublime too, right down to the little motorised arms that offered up the seatbelts when you sat in the front seats, just to save you the effort of having to reach back to find them. Of course, Dad could have achieved a similar effect in his Cavalier or Escort simply by training his children to pass him the belt every time he got in, but it's unlikely they'd have been as reliable as stout Mercedes engineering. Plus, the belt butler in the SEC wasn't likely to get you a visit from the NSPCC.

★ **Years on sale:** 1981-91
★ **Engine:** V8 cylinder, fuel-injected, 4973cc, mounted at the front
★ **Bodywork:** two-door, four-seater coupé
★ **Top speed:** 142mph
★ **0-60mph acceleration time:** 7.9sec
★ **Maximum power:** 245bhp
★ **Original price:** £28,700

Connoisseur's choice or poverty pick? Even more awesome in sheer power is the 300bhp 560SEC, but the base model 380SEC or 420SEC has V8 smoothness aplenty by any standards – cheaper to run with very little loss of face to be suffered!

FACT: The 500SEC once appeared on a postage stamp in South Korea. No, really.

Porsche 911

The Porsche 911 was announced in 1963 but for real jet-set appeal, and the drooling admiration of '80s Dad, it's the 911s of the Yuppie era that you need to look at, and there's a very clear spec that they needed to be in. The paintwork had to be bright red, an attention-grabbing colour that might as well have had 'I've just got my bonus and sod the rest of you' embossed into it. The factory called it Guards Red. City Trader's Braces would have been closer to the mark. The interior, by contrast, should have been black. Leather was nice, especially if it came with the paint-matching red piping, but the standard pinstripe seats perfectly matched the driver's suit as he drove to work.

So equipped, the 911 became as much an '80s icon as Kelly Le Brock and weirdly motionless synthesiser duos. And yet it weathered the association with hair-gelled wine bar weasels and lived to fight on, just as it had survived Porsche's own attempts to replace it with the 928. This is all the more remarkable when you think how weird and outdated its rear-engined design actually was by the time the Reagan-Thatcher era arrived.

But Porsche stuck with it, constantly fettling and fiddling with a layout that should have been obsolete years before, and yet which 911 fans loved for its perversity. Porsche's stubborn persistence with hanging the engine behind the car was best summed up by *Top Gear* presenter and long-time 911 nut Richard Hammond when he wrote, 'If you or I stubbed a toe on the bedside table every time we got up in the morning, we would move the table. A Porsche engineer would redesign their foot.'

★ **Years on sale:** 1974-89 (second-generation cars)
★ **Engine:** flat-six cylinder, fuel-injected, 2687-3164cc, mounted at the back
★ **Bodywork:** two-door, 2+2 coupé, Targa or cabriolet
★ **Top speed:** 152mph (911 Carrera 3.2)
★ **0-60mph acceleration time:** 6.1sec (911 Carrera 3.2)
★ **Maximum power:** 231bhp (911 Carrera 3.2)
★ **Original price:** £7393 (911S 2.7-litre Targa in 1974)

Connoisseur's choice or poverty pick? It's Porsches for courses in the style stakes, for there was no cabriolet until 1982, but the definitive 911 of the 1980s boom was the post-1983 Carrera with the 3.2-litre motor.

FACT: 911s may have been around since 1963, but until the 40th anniversary special edition of 2003 very few of them had a badge on the back that actually said '911'.

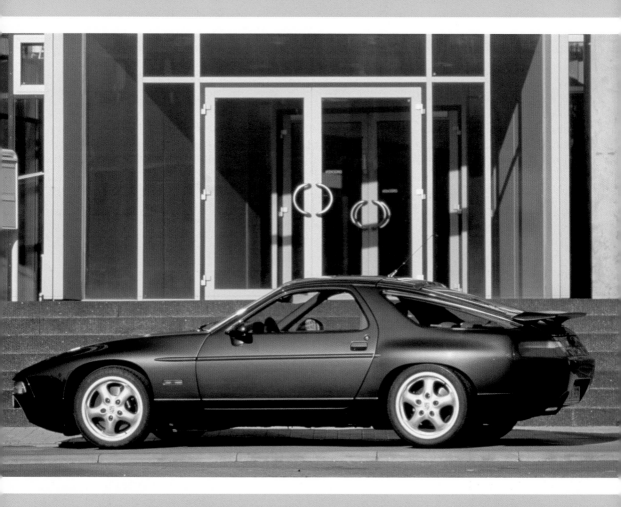

Porsche 928

At the dawn of the 1970s, Porsche's model line-up consisted of the 911 and a strange mongrel called the VW-Porsche 914. That was it. The company wisely decided that a brand-new car might be in order to broaden their range and, eventually, to step into the 911's shoes when its popularity waned. They sold a lot of cars in America and Americans liked V8s, so that's the sort of engine it would have. And since fitting such a massive engine 911-style at the back would do funny things to the handling, this new car would be front-engined and packed with high technology.

Development of Projekt 928 pressed on in such secrecy that Porsche bought some tatty old Audis and Opels and grafted their bodies onto 928 chassis so no one could tell what they were up to before, at the 1977 Geneva Motor Show, the finished car was revealed to the world. And the world said, What the bloody hell is that?

The 928's egg-like styling was controversial, with those flip-forward headlights and that strangely fat bottom, but there was no faulting the engineering, nor the attention to detail inside, which included instruments that moved with the adjustable steering wheel, extendable armrests in the doors and sun visors for the people in the back. Sadly some Porsche fans saw the lavish 928 as a sign that the company was going soft and fiercely stood by the 911 that it could have replaced. So, whilst the 928 was fabulous, it lived for 18 years whilst the 911 is still going strong at 45.

- ★ **Years on sale:** 1977-95
- ★ **Engine:** V8 cylinder, fuel-injected, 4474-5397cc, mounted at the front
- ★ **Bodywork:** two-door, four-seater coupé
- ★ **Top speed:** 168mph (S4)
- ★ **0-60mph acceleration time:** 5.4sec (GTS)
- ★ **Maximum power:** 350bhp (GTS)
- ★ **Original price:** £18,499 (S1)

Connoisseur's choice or poverty pick? No need, in the real world, to pay the premium for the final-incarnation GTS; even an S2 will give 158mph, and near 20mpg, with nothing lacking in the image department.

FACT: Porsche built a one-off full four-seater version of the 928, as a 75th birthday present for company emperor Ferry Porsche. It was 10 inches longer than normal and also had raised 'sightline' edges to the front wings, so that Herr Porsche could park without dinging its handmade panels.

Triumph Stag

It's the name that does it. Imagine you're in a 1970s dream world, there's a picture of Leslie Phillips on the wall and you are planning a run out to the countryside, smoothly suffixed with the words, 'Let's take the Stag.' Except that actually, it should have been spelt 'Staaaaaag'. Moustache twirling compulsory.

There was something very raffish about this handsome British cruiser, and not a little naughty. Although when it came to the car itself, this 'naughtiness' most commonly manifested itself in little foibles like the engine packing up again. It was a troublesome bit of kit, much given to boiling over, and Stag lovers have often bemoaned Triumph for creating this flaky V8 from scratch when they could have used a tough and proven eight-cylinder engine from their colleagues down the road at Rover.

Triumph experts will point out that it wasn't as simple as that,

and that Rover had no engines to spare, which does beg the question, why didn't Triumph spend their money on building a duplicate Rover V8 production line, instead of blowing it all on a hot-headed waste of space that royally knackered the reputation of this otherwise wonderful car? Still, at least when it was working the rumbling, bass-heavy Stag sounded truly, utterly fabulous. Almost as fabulous as saying its name.

★ **Years on sale:** 1970-77
★ **Engine:** V8 cylinder, twin-carburettor, 2997cc, mounted at the front
★ **Bodywork:** two-door, four-seater coupé
★ **Top speed:** 118mph
★ **0-60mph acceleration time:** 9.7sec
★ **Maximum power:** 145bhp
★ **Original price:** £2441

Connoisseur's choice or poverty pick? The Mk2, from 1973 onwards, was vastly improved with a more reliable engine, a better interior and alloy wheels. Today, as when it was new, the Stag is even more usable with the optional hardtop.

> **FACT: The Stag was the first British car to feature an inertia switch which cut off fuel in the event of an accident. Otherwise, it wasn't particularly well equipped. The seats were upholstered in plain vinyl, the soft top was manually operated, and the wheel covers appeared to be made of tinfoil.**

RANCH-STYLE (Bungalow)

Chevrolet Corvette Sting Ray

The original Chevrolet Corvette of 1953 was undoubtedly a pretty thing, but with a saloon car chassis, wheezing six-cylinder engine and automatic gearbox it was about as lively as a game of Scrabble. Buyers weren't impressed, and Chevy almost gave up on its attempts to make a sports car until some bright spark suggested bolting their new V8 engine and a manual gearbox into the Corvette's fibreglass hull. Suddenly they were back in the game, and so began the Vette's glorious evolution, which hit a new high in 1963 with this, the Sting Ray.

This was a remarkable-looking thing, what with its rotating headlamps, dramatically slotted bonnet, extravagant gills in the front wings and an unusual rear window with a bar running right down the middle. But the things that influenced its designer were equally remarkable, including the Jaguar E-type in his garage at home and a mako shark he'd caught whilst out fishing. In fact, in retrospect he might have got a bit carried away, because the following year the Sting Ray's design was toned down and weird details like the split

rear window were ditched. But the hearty 5.4-litre V8 remained and a Corvette legend was born.

All of which wasn't much use to Dad, of course, since the Vette was never sold in the UK and by comparison his Cortina seemed to have been modelled not on Jaguars and sharks, but by looking at a corned beef sandwich.

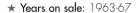

- ★ **Years on sale:** 1963-67
- ★ **Engine:** V8 cylinder, single- or triple-carburettor/fuel-injected, 5356/6999cc, mounted at the front
- ★ **Bodywork:** two-door, two-seater coupé and roadster
- ★ **Top speed:** 145mph (7-litre)
- ★ **0-60mph acceleration time:** 5.6sec (7-litre)
- ★ **Maximum power:** 435bhp (7-litre)
- ★ **Original price:** £3,323 (in 1964)

Connoisseur's choice or poverty pick? About 20 of these Corvettes were fitted with the legendary L88 engine, offering no less than 560bhp and 170mph for sports-car racing. They're worth at least $1m a pop now. The pre-'64 split-window coupé is prized by collectors. Try anything else – you're fairly sure not to be disappointed.

> *FACT: The Corvette name was suggested by one of Chevrolet's advertising staff and came from a type of small, agile warship.*

Ford Mustang

The Ford Mustang was a landmark moment in the history of the car, not for its engineering - far from it actually - but for the marketing thought behind it. Technically, the original 'Stang was a pretty simple thing, largely based on run-of-the-mill saloon car bits but garnished with one hell of a handsome body. And if a car looks good, it's probably going to sell, as indeed the Mustang did, shifting one million cars in its first 18 months and thus becoming the fastest-selling car ever made.

But the genius of the 'Stang wasn't just that it dressed up ordinary parts to look fantastic, it was the way it let you have the car you wanted. Certainly, you could have plumped for the basic two-door hardtop running a straight-six engine miserably titled the 'Thriftpower', but what you really wanted – and what Ford, with the Mustang's ever-bigger options list, was happy to sell you – was a convertible or a fastback with a V8 and a fancier interior.

With the original Mustang, Ford had, for the first time, made the options list a drool-fest in its own right. Unless, that is, you were a British dad, in which case you couldn't buy a Mustang and had to content yourself with considering optional mudflaps on a Capri.

* ★ **Years on sale:** 1964-69 (Mk1)
* ★ **Engine:** straight-six and V8 cylinder, single-carburettor/fuel-injected, 2799-6997cc, mounted at the front
* ★ **Bodywork:** two-door, four-seater hardtop coupé, fastback coupé and convertible
* ★ **Top speed:** 135mph (GT-390)
* ★ **0-60mph acceleration time:** 6sec (GT-390)
* ★ **Maximum power:** 390bhp (GT-390)
* ★ **Original price:** £2414 (289 hardtop, 4.7-litre in 1965)

Connoisseur's choice or poverty pick? The Mustang is at its purest from the 1964-69 era, and with one of the V8 engines, though not necessarily the 390bhp engine of the McQueen *Bullitt* car. The six-cylinder cars ain't quick. Body style choice to suit, just as when new.

> **FACT:** Ford has always made the Mustang affordable by basing it on other cars. In the '80s it shared a chassis with the Ford Thunderbird, whilst the current one is distantly related to the Jag S-type.

Newest version of America's most exciting car

'56 FORD THUNDERBIRD

Ford Thunderbird

You know a car is destined to be a legend if it's immortalised in song and, thanks to the Beach Boys, the Ford Thunderbird was. Not something that ever happened to the Austin Maxi, even though Morrissey probably thought about it. Of course, the other thing that helps to cement a car in the popular imagination is a rocking good name, and here the Thunderbird was mightily well equipped to echo through the ages.

That evocative badge was the result of a competition within Ford to find the right handle for its new car, and the man who came up with the winning entry, a designer called Alden Giberson, was given $95 and – oh, the decadence! – a new pair of trousers as a reward for his trouble.

If that sounds disappointing, it's not as much of a letdown as that experienced by anyone who thought the Thunderbird was a sports car because, despite appearances, it wasn't. Instead it was what Ford called a 'personal luxury car', something which was meant to look smart and sporty, but without compromising comfort. In which case, job done. At least until your daddy took it away.

* **Years on sale:** 1955-66 (first four generations)
* **Engine:** V8 cylinder, single-carburettor, 4785-6965cc, mounted at the front
* **Bodywork:** two-door, four-seater hardtop coupé and convertible
* **Top speed:** 135mph (1965-7 427)
* **0-60mph acceleration time:** 6sec (1965-7 427)
* **Maximum power:** 425bhp (1965-7 427)
* **Original price:** not sold in UK

Connoisseur's choice or poverty pick? The sexiest Thunderbirds are from 1961-66, the third and fourth generations nicknamed the 'Bullet Birds' and 'Flair Birds' by fanatics.

> **FACT: Walking round the Paris Motor Show, a Ford boss asked his designer why they weren't working on sporty, European-looking cars. We are, fibbed the designer, then snuck off to phone his studio and tell them to get some Euro-style designs ready for when the boss got back to Detroit. One of them became the Thunderbird.**

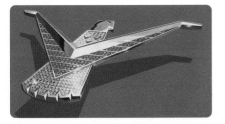

Pontiac Trans Am

Naming the mightiest of their Firebird range after a great American racing series obviously seemed like a good idea to Pontiac, and clearly one that justified the per-car royalty they had to pay to the Sports Car Club of America who owned it. And by God it was worth every cent, because that strangely abbreviated name became evocative and famous across the world, almost entirely down to the car rather than because of a bunch of people driving round in circles.

In all its various forms, the Trans Am was an icon, even though it wasn't what you'd call complicated. The V8 was big, the chassis was simple, the whole thing gave the impression that, if it was a person, it would be the kind of dumb cousin lover that would have a good time by loosing off a coupla handguns into the air. Sophisticated it was not. Not unless it was black, had an oscillating red light across its nose and regularly talked in camp tones to a tight-trousered man who, so they told us, did not exist. Yes, the most famous Trans Am of all was a

1982 model called KITT that was far cleverer not just than any other Pontiac of its type but than any other car. Rumours that they cut out the sequence in one episode where the car reverted to type and shouted, 'Screw you, Mikey, I'm gonna pound some beers and then go shoot at the moon…' are completely unfounded.

★ **Years on sale:** 1969-2002 (all four generations)
★ **Engine:** V8 cylinder, single-carburettor, 4785-6965cc, mounted at the front
★ **Bodywork:** two-door, four-seater coupé
★ **Top speed:** 132mph (7.5-litre, 1973-76)
★ **0-60mph acceleration time:** 5.4sec (7.5-litre, 1973-76)
★ **Maximum power:** 310bhp (7.5-litre, 1973-76)
★ **Original price:** £8014 (in 1978)

Connoisseur's choice or poverty pick? There's a myriad choices when it comes to Trans Ams, let alone all the other versions of the Pontiac Firebird. Muscle car fans rate the mid-70s cars as the best, but *Knight Rider*-era cars have more resonance, and some can be extremely hairy machines…

FACT: The Firebird was finally axed in 2002, and has never really been replaced, despite the successful revival of its old foe the Ford Mustang and the imminent return of its sister car, the Chevrolet Camaro.

SCREEN DREAMS

DeLorean DMC-12

Funny old car, the DeLorean. Originally touted as an admirable 'ethical sports car', it finally entered production as a bizarre stainless-steel novelty with a gasping V6 engine on a thinly disguised Lotus Esprit chassis. Shortly after which the car itself became secondary to the antics of its creator, John Z. DeLorean, who managed to twist a load of money out of the British government in return for siting his factory in Northern Ireland, and then got busted by the Feds for his involvement in a drug-trafficking ring.

But though its creator's life was apparently taken from a Hollywood movie plot, the DMC-12 itself would have faded into obscurity had it not been for the patronage of an actual Hollywood movie that made it an icon across the world.

When the producers of *Back to the Future* started looking for something to turn into a time machine, their first idea was to base it on a refrigerator. But, fearing kids would start climbing into their parents' fridges, they changed their minds and settled on the DeLorean, mainly because it looked like a spaceship. One massive box-office smash (and two sequels) later, the DMC-12 was a star. But let's not forget that it was also an awful car. That running gag from *Back to the Future* where Marty bangs his head on the

open door? It was improvised on set because, like many DeLoreans, the prop car's lousy door struts wouldn't keep it open properly. And that's the DeLorean for you. A movie icon, but also a bit of a joke.

★ **Years on sale:** 1981-83
★ **Engine:** V6 cylinder, fuel-injected, 2849cc, mounted at the rear
★ **Bodywork:** two-door, two-seater coupé
★ **Top speed:** 121mph
★ **0-60mph acceleration time:** 10.2sec
★ **Maximum power:** 130bhp
★ **Original price:** not sold in the UK

Connoisseur's choice or poverty pick? A batch of 20 right-hand drive DeLoreans were made for a doomed assault on the UK market. One would be worth snapping up, especially as its performance is much brisker without the US-market exhaust emission equipment that the left-hand drive examples had to have.

> **FACT: DeLorean's brand-new factory near Belfast still stands today, but is now occupied by a French company that makes engine parts and alloy wheels.**

Dodge Charger

The Dodge Charger muscle car started life in 1966 as a lumpy-looking fastback that enjoyed moderate success in NASCAR racing. In 1968, however, it was restyled into a more elegant coupé, complete with stylish buttresses either side of the back window. Its designer thought these would improve the aerodynamics on track, although as it turned out they made things worse. More significantly, a '68 Charger kicked off the car's screen career, starring as the bad guy's wheels in the movie *Bullitt*. Then, in 1979, Warner Brothers premiered a new TV show about two good ol' boys and a bright orange '69 Charger called the General Lee which soon became one of the most famous cars in the world.

Estimates vary on how many Dodges were written off in six years of filming *The Dukes of Hazzard* but some put it as high as 300, and this might explain why the show's producers started combing California, leaving notes on parked Chargers begging their owners to sell. They set up a permanent workshop to rebuild smashed cars, and even resorted to reusing stunt footage before, in 1985, the big-budget show was canned. There was a happy ending for some

Charger fans though, because four years after the show wrapped, members of the Dodge Charger Register were invited to Warner Brothers' lot and, to their amazement, led into a field containing 17 battered General Lee stunt cars which the studio agreed to sell to them.

- ★ **Years on sale:** 1968-70
- ★ **Engine:** V8 cylinder, single-carburettor, 5210-7206cc, mounted at the front
- ★ **Bodywork:** two-door, four-seater coupé
- ★ **Top speed:** 156mph (R/T)
- ★ **0-60mph acceleration time:** 4.6sec (R/T)
- ★ **Maximum power:** 425bhp (R/T)
- ★ **Original price:** not sold in the UK

Connoisseur's choice or poverty pick? The R/T, standing for Road and Track, is certainly the daddy here, with its 6.9-litre engine, although the less powerful standard Chargers won't leave you wanting for punch and unbeatable muscle car styling.

FACT: John Schneider, who played Bo Duke, says he did 60 per cent of the onscreen driving himself, the rest tackled by 20 stunt drivers. 'The truth is,' he said, 'once you've seen a 3500lb car hit the ground at 50mph from 20ft in the air, you really don't want to try it yourself.'

Ferrari 308 GTS

See a Ferrari 308 these days and it looks like an '80s throwback, the kind of car that can only be driven whilst wearing a crumpled linen suit and Ray-Bans Wayfarers. But back in the actual '80s this was the very definition of cool, not least because it was used by television's favourite thickly moustachioed private investigator, Magnum PI.

As with a lot of those hilariously overblown Glen A. Larson TV shows from that era, the actual details of Magnum PI seem a bit strange in retrospect; chiefly that he was a Vietnam veteran who lived on the estate of a mysterious author in the company of an uptight man with an unconvincing English accent and he had a mate who for some vague but often convenient reason flew a helicopter. Oh yeah, and the whole thing was set on Hawaii, mainly

because the studio had just finished making *Hawaii Five-O* in the same place and wanted another production to make use of its facilities there.

But unless you're glued to reruns on top cable channel UK '80s Gold 7, the specifics of Magnum PI are irrelevant. All you need to know is that he had one of these Ferrari 308s and at the time that made everyone else want one too.

* ★ **Years on sale:** 1977-81
* ★ **Engine:** V8 cylinder, quadruple-carburettor/fuel-injected, 2921cc, mounted in the centre
* ★ **Bodywork:** two-door, two-seater Targa coupé
* ★ **Top speed:** 155mph
* ★ **0-60mph acceleration time:** 6.5sec
* ★ **Maximum power:** 250bhp
* ★ **Original price:** £15,499

Connoisseur's choice or poverty pick? In this form, the 308 wasn't around for long, but the fuel-injected 308 GTSi, made between 1981 and 1985, might be more reliable anyway.

> **FACT: Magnum producers were going to use a Porsche 928, but asked the factory to make one with a bigger sunroof so everyone could see Tom Selleck's luxuriant moustache during the aerial tracking shots. Porsche refused, so the TV people got in this Targa-roofed Ferrari.**

Ford Gran Torino

The Ford Gran Torino was an unexceptional range of cars, and even the more rakish coupé version just wasn't as cool as Ford's own Mustang. That is until some TV producers decided to give one to a lead character in a new buddy-buddy cop show. *Starsky & Hutch* first aired in 1975, and pretty soon it became clear that the show should have been called *Starsky & Hutch & That Red Car With The Big White Stripe Down The Side.*

David Starsky's distinctive Gran Torino became one of the most recognisable faces from the programme and, unlike David Soul, one that didn't keep releasing bloody records. The cars themselves came direct from Ford, but the stripe was added by the TV studio, at least until someone back in Detroit realised there was capital to be had from this starring role and authorised a factory-built run of replicas for sale to the general public. To this day the colour scheme makes it one of the most recognisable cars in the world, even if, according to Hutch, it looked like a 'striped tomato'.

★ **Years on sale:** 1972-76
★ **Engine:** straight-six cylinder, single-carburettor, 4097cc or V8 cylinder, single-carburettor, 4950-7030cc, mounted at the front
★ **Bodywork:** two-door, four-seater coupé or four-door, four-seater 'hardtop' saloon
★ **Top speed:** 118mph (7-litre)
★ **0-60mph acceleration time:** 7.7sec (7-litre)
★ **Maximum power:** 246bhp (7-litre)
★ **Original price:** not sold in the UK

Connoisseur's choice or poverty pick? In spring 1976, 1000 special-edition *Starsky & Hutch* Gran Torinos rolled off Ford's Chicago production line. They've since become highly collectable, although checking the chassis number against factory records is the only way to avoid a fake.

> **FACT: Some of the cars used in the TV series had vinyl bench seats in the front. These were hastily replaced with bucket seats after the two stars kept sliding into each other during fast cornering for the cameras.**

Volvo P1800

The most curious thing about the P1800 is that Volvo made it at all. It's not as if they were exactly known for their prowess in making sports cars, and their one previous attempt, a cute roadster called the P1900, had been a complete disaster. Nonetheless, in 1960 they had another crack, contracted Jensen in Britain to build it for them, and found things turned out rather better, especially when they were asked to supply a white P1800 for a new TV series called *The Saint*.

Sensing plugging potential, Volvo jumped at the chance where Jaguar, whose massive MkX saloon had been the TV company's original choice of prop car, said no. It turned out to be a smart move from the Swedes, since this TV series gave Volvo's unexpected sports car enormous publicity. Not just in the UK either because the *The Saint* was a rare example of a British TV show sold to the US, alerting an American audience to the sports car from a company that didn't normally bother with such things. No wonder

that when they began making *The Return of the Saint* with Ian Ogilvy, Jaguar had a sudden change of heart and happily supplied the production with an XJS for the lead character. Shame for them that the sequel show only lasted for one series. Dah!

* **Years on sale:** 1960-72
* **Engine:** straight-four cylinder, twin-carburettor/fuel-injected, 1778/1985cc, mounted at the front
* **Bodywork:** two-door, two-seater coupé
* **Top speed:** 110mph (1800E)
* **0-60mph acceleration time:** 9.6sec (1800E)
* **Maximum power:** 120bhp (1800E)
* **Original price:** £1837 (P1800)

Connoisseur's choice or poverty pick? Quality vastly improved with the P1800S of 1963, and power was upped with the 1800E, but the earliest cars – with their boomerang-style half-bumpers – are the classic original.

> **FACT:** During **The Saint's** lengthy run, **Volvo** tweaked the **P1800's** design, making the car on TV obsolete. The producers got round this by writing a scene where Templar's car exploded and then another in which he bought a new one.

THE LEGENDS

Ferrari Daytona

This, though few knew it at the time, would be Ferrari's last front-engined, two-seater GT supercar for some time. As such, it represented the pinnacle of what they knew about shoving a Gods of War V12 under the long, flowing bonnet of a beautiful machine meant for monstering entire continents in an afternoon.

The 4.4-litre engine was more powerful than ever and, allied to a five-speed gearbox which was still something of a novelty in those days, a fit Daytona could gallop up to 180mph. In fact, such was this car's mighty strength, it could soar past Britain's still-new 70mph limit without even changing out of second.

But the best thing about the Daytona was the way it looked. Even by Ferrari's pretty bloody lovely standards, this was a classic and, because it manages to be both of its time and yet somehow refuses to date, it remains gruntingly gorgeous to this day. Obviously your dad wanted one in inverse proportion to how much he could afford one – lots versus not at all – but there was some small comfort for father when, in 1976, Rover introduced their

SD1 executive car, which brilliantly and shamelessly nicked many styling elements off the recently defunct Ferrari. Yes, it wasn't an actual Ferrari, but your mum wasn't actually Brigitte Bardot and he still loved her, didn't he?

★ **Years on sale:** 1968-73
★ **Engine:** V12 cylinder, six carburettors, 4390cc, mounted at the front
★ **Bodywork:** two-door, two-seater coupé or roadster
★ **Top speed:** 174mph
★ **0-60mph acceleration time:** 5.4sec
★ **Maximum power:** 352bhp
★ **Original price:** £8563

Connoisseur's choice or poverty pick? There's obscenely valuable – that's the coupé – and then there's stratospheric – the Spyder, of which there are just 165 examples plus, of course, plenty of non-original conversions.

> **FACT: The Daytona had a resurgence in the '80s after Sonny Crockett drove one in sockless cop-fest Miami Vice. In fact Crockett's Daytona Spyder was a replica based on a Corvette and was later replaced with a genuine Testarossa.**

Jaguar E-type

Almost perfect for disparaging cod-Freudian analysis of why we like sports cars, the long, narrow, slightly tubular E-type has been the subject of more flowery words on its appearance than almost any car in the world. But there's good reason for that, because it's the perfect example of what we imagine a sports car should be.

Some people think they should be coupés, others favour convertibles. The E was both. Everyone wants mighty power from a many-cylindered engine, and this car had that in spades. Racing pedigree is nice too, and the E-type's XK engine was the same as that in the C- and D-type racers, whilst the car itself had a respectable racing career of its own. Another box checked.

But most of all, we want a sports car to be beautiful, and by golly the E-type was and still is. The secret to its charms isn't just the lovely proportions and the exquisite details, it's that the whole body is perfectly curvaceous, like something formed in nature rather than contrived in a design studio.

As sports cars go, what you're looking at here is the textbook.

★ **Years on sale:** 1961-75
★ **Engine:** straight-six cylinder, single-carburettor, 3781/4235cc or V12 cylinder, quadruple-carburettor, 5343cc, mounted at the front
★ **Bodywork:** two-door, two- or 2+2-seater coupé; two-door, two-seater roadster
★ **Top speed:** 150mph (V12)
★ **0-60mph acceleration time:** 6.4sec (V12)
★ **Maximum power:** 246bhp (V12)
★ **Original price:** £2159

Connoisseur's choice or poverty pick? Real Jag anoraks rate the 'Series 1-and-a-half' roadster as the acme of the E-type because it has the original shape and 4.2-litre motor. But the V12 is the only 'E' that can really hit 150mph.

> **FACT:** After the bad reception for the XJS, Jaguar tried to get back to the E-type formula with a secret 'F-type' project, codenamed XJ41. It dragged on through the '80s, getting fatter and less sporty, until they had the sense to kill it off.

Lamborghini Miura

Whilst not the very first mid-engined Italian car – De Tomaso pipped them to the post on that one – Lamborghini's Miura is certainly the most famous early example of the racing-based layout we know today. What's all the more remarkable about this car is that it was created by a very young team, working off their wits. The early plans were sketched out in chalk on the workshop floor, and they weren't afraid to borrow good ideas, hence the Miura's engine sits across the car rather than lengthways, inspired – quite bizarrely – by the Mini. To showcase the brave new layout, Lamborghini showed off a bare chassis during 1965 and people placed orders for it, even before seeing Marcello Gandini's achingly gorgeous body on top.

The Miura was reportedly even more exciting to drive than it was to look at, not least because at high speed its nose went terrifyingly light, a problem made even worse the lower the fuel got in its front-mounted tank. Yes, you had to have gentlemen's equipment the size of watermelons to really master a Miura, but by God your dad would have loved to have tried.

★ **Years on sale:** 1966-72
★ **Engine:** V12 cylinder, quadruple-carburettor, 3929cc, mounted in the centre
★ **Bodywork:** two-door, two-seater coupé
★ **Top speed:** 180mph (SV)
★ **0-60mph acceleration time:** 6.5sec approx (SV)
★ **Maximum power:** 385bhp (SV)
★ **Original price:** £8050

Connoisseur's choice or poverty pick? The scorching SV is the fastest of a sizzling line-up, but there are so few Miuras around (only 765 were made) that most of us wouldn't mind which one we had to drive to Morrisons in.

> **FACT: The curve in the Miura's side windows is there so that when you stand in front of the car with its doors open it looks like the horns of a bull. Nice touch.**

FOUR BIG SEATS, TWO LONG DOORS, ONE FAT CHEQUE

Ferrari 400

This, it must be said, is not one of Ferrari's finest moments. It might have run a version of the V12 engine from the iconic Daytona, but in all other respects this was not a thoroughbred. For a start, the design was upright and barely skimmed the edges of beautiful, especially since the 400 often appeared to be sagging downwards at the back, like a slowly sinking canal boat. An elegant Daytona-alike it was not.

It upset Ferrari fans in other ways, too, chiefly by offering an automatic gearbox which, worse still, was enthusiastically embraced by a majority of buyers. This spoke volumes about who was buying this four-seater: most likely wealthy families who liked the idea of keeping a Ferrari but at the same time needed to calm down and think of the children. Although really, if you'd been that mindful of your offspring, maybe you'd have settled for a Merc S-class and a Dino 246 for weekends. That way they could have said, 'My dad's got a Ferrari' and not had to ride around in this mongrel.

★ **Years on sale:** 1976-85
★ **Engine:** V12 cylinder, six carburettors/fuel-injected, 4823cc, mounted at the front
★ **Bodywork:** two-door, four-seater saloon
★ **Top speed:** 156mph (400 auto)
★ **0-60mph acceleration time:** 8sec (400 auto)
★ **Maximum power:** 315bhp (400i)
★ **Original price:** £22,464 (400GT)

Connoisseur's choice or poverty pick? Not much fancied by Ferrari fans, these cars go for a song, yet they offer a lot of Italian machine for the money. The fuel-injected 400i is the better of the two, but there is also the later 412 which has a 5-litre engine and many other improvements.

> **FACT: Fans may sneer at clutchless 400s but actual customers disagreed. Ferrari sold 27 right-hand-drive 400s with manual transmissions but 137 as automatics.**

Lamborghini Espada

In line with Lamborghini's tradition of bull-related names, Espada came from the Spanish word for the sword used by bullfighters, which seemed appropriate because this was a remarkable piece of weaponry. Yes, it had four seats but it was also a Lamborghini, and for the most part that second quality won through.

The engine was the same bellowing V12 that went into their full fat supercars and, though it wasn't as elegant as a Miura, the Espada did manage to be massively and brutally dramatic, with its huge overhangs and tantalising details like the race-car-style intake slots in the bonnet. Those were actually there to feed fresh air to the people inside, but it speaks volumes about this four-person cruise missile that Lambo had managed to dress up even functional items to look sexy.

The interior was equally racy, with its wood-rimmed steering wheel, vast platter of dials and – in later models – a dashboard that curved round towards the driver so he could pretend he was in a fighter plane. But a fighter plane with his kids in the back.

★ **Years on sale:** 1968-78
★ **Engine:** V12 cylinder, six carburettors, 3929cc, mounted at the front
★ **Bodywork:** two-door, four-seater coupé
★ **Top speed:** 155mph
★ **0-60mph acceleration time:** 7.8sec
★ **Maximum power:** 350bhp
★ **Original price:** £10,295

Connoisseur's choice or poverty pick? A truly fantastic four-seater, with later versions just having the edge in the power stakes by adding an extra 25bhp. These ones also have a better cabin, which makes using your Espada easier.

> **FACT: Not exactly lacking drama, the Espada could have been even more exciting if they'd persisted with the original plan to give it massive gullwing doors.**

Maserati Indy

Supercars are all well and good, but not so handy if you've got a growing family. Fortunately at the end of the 1960s, Maserati stepped into the breach by adding this to their ever-growing range.

It was a car with all the proper performance of an Italian exotic – late 4.9-litre versions could top 170 mph, yet it had four seats and the top-notch interior trimmings you'd expect from a mile-monstering GT. Early versions even had an instrument pod on the driver's side, and then a mirror of that same pod on the passenger side, although disappointingly it contained only a clock rather than auxiliary speed dials that would allow you to pretend you were co-pilot.

Yes, the Indy wasn't quite as elegant as its Ghibli brother, but then your dad probably didn't look as fresh-faced now he had to look after kids. Although it's safe to say one of those would probably have ironed out some of his wrinkles.

★ **Years on sale:** 1969-75
★ **Engine:** V8 cylinder, quadruple-carburettor, 4136-4930cc, mounted at the front
★ **Bodywork:** two-door, four-seater coupé
★ **Top speed:** 165mph (5-litre)
★ **0-60mph acceleration time:** 7sec approx (5-litre)
★ **Maximum power:** 335bhp (5-litre)
★ **Original price:** £8320

Connoisseur's choice or poverty pick? The 5-litre was a special-order-only car, aimed at the wealthy speed-freak dad, but the 4.7-litre car also shares an engine with the iconic Ghibli and so is still fairly sensational. The Indy has no separate chassis, and is rust-prone.

FACT: When the Indy was current, all Maseratis sold in the UK were rewired by a London specialist to make sure they met safety rules and could hope to withstand the damp British climate.

Mercedes-Benz 450 SLC

Everyone knows the Mercedes SL of 1971, the upright yet rather louche roadster that starred in *Dallas* and eventually became one of the most enduring cars Merc has ever made, lasting right up until 1989. Jolly good it was too. But the lesser-known SLC is the thinking man's version of that car, an unusually stretched version with a fixed roof and – crucially for the family man – proper seating in the back instead of that ludicrous leather-slathered torture slot you got on the roadster.

Of course, the SLC wasn't quite as classically elegant as its soft-top sister, but it had a certain stoutly Germanic appeal for the more discerning. And since it lived a far shorter life than the SL, shuffling off at the dawn of the '80s when the bigger SEC coupés came along, it never received the modernising touches of its brethren, so that if you see one today it looks like a product of its time, all chrome details and slightly old-fashioned wheels. There

was a sort of brilliant faded glamour about this car, as if its ideal driver would be a gravel-voiced, languidly smoking headscarf wearer, on the way to meet an illicit gentleman lover whilst the kids were at school. Who knows, maybe that was indeed your mum. Or even, perhaps, your dad.

★ **Years on sale:** 1972-80
★ **Engine:** V8 cylinder, fuel-injected, 4520cc, mounted at the front
★ **Bodywork:** two-door, four-seater coupé
★ **Top speed:** 135mph
★ **0-60mph acceleration time:** 9sec
★ **Maximum power:** 225bhp
★ **Original price:** £10,435

Connoisseur's choice or poverty pick? A wide range of other engines in this body style, although it's quite a heavy car for a 2.8-litre straight-six to manage. The 450 is undoubtedly the best of the SLCs, likely to have the best specification…and is no doubt the most expensive to run.

FACT: Given its smoothly urbane nature, it's surprising to learn that Merc's factory rally team competed with SLCs for a while, and they weren't bad either. One even won the Ivory Coast Rally. Blimey.

Rolls-Royce Camargue

The Italian design studio Pininfarina has been responsible for some of the most beautiful, elegant, eye-pleasing cars ever made. And this. Which is none of those things. In fact, it's a wonder that when you look in the dictionary under 'leviathan' it doesn't say 'see Rolls-Royce Camargue'. The sad thing is that Rolls was convinced to shun its in-house stylists and use an outside designer for this car after seeing Pininfarina's work on a one-off Bentley, which was indeed rather gracious and pretty. But when it came to making a full production model out of it, things appeared to go awry, and in anything but profile this monstrous coupé seems lumpen and silly, as if its massive body has been accidentally fitted to the chassis of a slightly smaller car.

In fact, the underneath parts came from the Silver Shadow saloon and this explains why, despite being a coupé, the Camargue has space for four people inside. Perhaps this is why ever-sensible Dad would lust after one rather than some frivolous and cramped two-seater. Because it was the preposterous millionaire's plaything that let the whole family come along for the ride.

The Camargue's geekiest claim to fame is as first Rolls designed in metric units. Although to look at it you might assume that, whilst the Italians delivered the plans in centimetres, the British still tried to assemble it in inches.

★ **Years on sale:** 1977-86
★ **Engine:** V8 cylinder, single-carburettor, 6750cc, mounted at the front
★ **Bodywork:** two-door, four-seater saloon
★ **Top speed:** 119mph
★ **0-60mph acceleration time:** 10sec
★ **Maximum power:** not disclosed but stated as 'adequate'
★ **Original price:** £29,250

Connoisseur's choice or poverty pick? Phenomenally expensive to buy new and to run today; there was only one model, although the trim and colours of some later ones can be a touch dubious. i.e. ghastly.

FACT: The Camargue was the first Rolls-Royce to have air-conditioning as standard. And not just any air-conditioning, but an automatic system that could blow a different temperature of air to different parts of the interior. Whizzy stuff for the '70s.

KEEP DOING THE POOLS, FATHER

Aston Martin Lagonda

If you want to know how radical but ultimately nuts the 1970s could be, have a closer look at this. Designed without compromise, or indeed anyone who could draw curves, the Lagonda was a lavish luxury saloon powered by a hearty V8 engine and slathered with a mass of interesting new technology. This included LCD instruments and touch-sensitive switches, but when the car was previewing in 1976, neither worked properly. The car finally went on sale in 1978, at which point they still didn't work.

Then Aston replaced the LCD gauges with even fancier cathode-ray tube screens and they, erm, didn't work either. Nonetheless, the car was surprisingly popular in the Middle East, presumably because buyers there had enough money to afford a fleet of other cars they could use when their Lagonda's dials had gone on the wonk again.

And for dreaming Dad, this was still an object of lust simply for its sheer drama and excitement. Although if he'd actually been able to afford one, he probably should have kept his Marina too, just in case the Aston went wrong.

★ **Years on sale:** 1978-90
★ **Engine:** V8 cylinder, quadruple-carburettor/fuel-injected, 5340cc, mounted at the front
★ **Bodywork:** four-door, four-seater saloon
★ **Top speed:** 145mph
★ **0-60mph acceleration time:** 8.4sec
★ **Maximum power:** 300bhp
★ **Original price:** £24,570

Connoisseur's choice or poverty pick? Another super-saloon that cost a king's ransom when new and today is rather unwanted in the classic car world. A 1987 facelift didn't improve on the Lagonda's crisp looks, so you might enjoy owning an earlier one.

> **FACT: On 29 April 1978 Aston called a press conference at Woburn Abbey and with great fanfare handed the first Lagonda to its new owners, Lord and Lady Tavistock. The car promptly suffered total electrical meltdown and refused to start.**

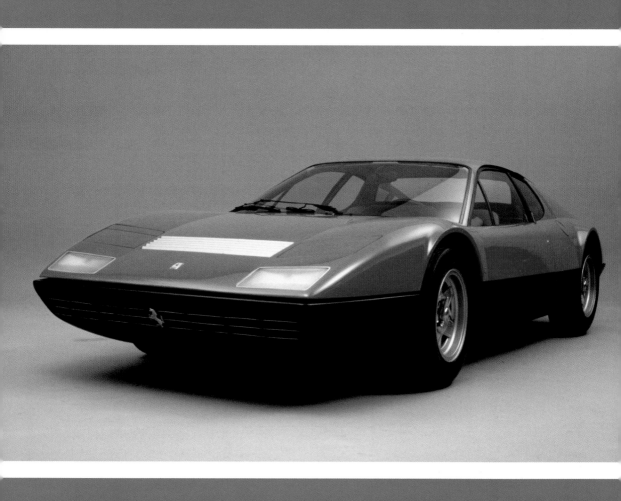

Ferrari Berlinetta Boxer

In the 1970s it wasn't just T. Rex versus Slade or the Pistols versus The Clash. For excitable, power-wowed kids everywhere (and their dads too) one of the best battles of the decade was Lamborghini Countach versus Ferrari Berlinetta Boxer. The Countach might have scored on sheer flamboyance, but the Ferrari was the prettier car and still looks good today in its own tough but stylish way. This is especially true if you see one without its lower half painted in matt black, which was very popular at the time but now looks so dated they might as well have wrapped the roof in cheesecloth.

Under that sweet skin, the Boxer was a departure for Ferrari, being their first mid-engined twelve-cylinder car. Up until that point the company had considered the front to be the safest place for their titanic V12 engines, but then the Boxer didn't actually have a V12. Instead, its two banks of six cylinders were laid flat, a format Ferrari had already tried in racing.

In theory this engine should have been lower, dropping the centre of gravity and making the car more stable, but in fact the Boxer had a reputation for biting back if you pushed it. Still, because in profile the flat engine's pistons pushed towards each

other like a boxer's gloves before a fight, at least it usefully contributed the car's name. Just in case you mistakenly thought it was a random tribute to Henry Cooper or something.

★ **Years on sale:** 1972-76
★ **Engine:** flat-12 cylinder, quadruple-carburettor/fuel-injected, 4942cc, mounted in the centre
★ **Bodywork:** two-door, two-seater coupé
★ **Top speed:** 188mph (512i)
★ **0-60mph acceleration time:** 5.2sec (512i)
★ **Maximum power:** 380bhp (512i)
★ **Original price:** £23,868

Connoisseur's choice or poverty pick? The car had been launched in 1972 as the 365 GT4 BB and it was given a new lease of life as the much-modernised Testarossa in 1984. They're all rare and desirable and very tricky to rate one above the other – it'll come down to personal taste.

> **FACT: The Boxer marked the end of an era, being the last Ferrari to ditch its extremely vocal Weber carburettors in favour of the more reliable, less polluting but somehow less characterful Bosch K-Jetronic fuel-injection.**

Lamborghini Countach

For a broad swathe of the 1970s and '80s, this was the poster king of supercars. Sure, Athena sold glossy prints of other cars alongside tennis girl scratching her bum, but the Countach was always going to take pride of place on any excitable young boy's bedroom wall. Chiefly this was because it looked so much more outrageous than any other car in the world.

Lamborghini could get away with such things because, being essentially a tractor builder made good, they had none of Ferrari's old money hang-ups about taste, style and staying true to a racing heritage. Lamborghini just appeared to sit down and think, What would an eight-year-old boy do? And then whatever silliness that was, they doubled it and added a million. This made the Countach the ultimate pools winner car. No real breeding, but by God it was out to have a good time.

As the years went by, the Countach got even more ludicrous, so much so that the 1974 original actually started to seem quite tame, especially compared to the ludicrous slats and spoilers of the 1988 'Anniversary' edition, designed by the man who went on to invent the equally mental Pagani Zonda. But whatever the model, the Countach was always bold, brash, unabashed and not a little vulgar. Basically, it was the car equivalent of Rod Stewart's leopard-print trousers.

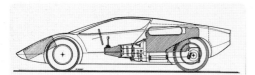

★ **Years on sale:** 1974-91
★ **Engine:** V12 cylinder, six carburettors/fuel-injected, 3929-5167cc, mounted in the centre
★ **Bodywork:** two-door, two-seater coupé
★ **Top speed:** 178mph (LP500S QV)
★ **0-60mph acceleration time:** 4.9sec (LP500S QV)
★ **Maximum power:** 455bhp (LP500S QV)
★ **Original price:** £17,285 (LP400)

Connoisseur's choice or poverty pick? You can't beat the sharp-edged style of the original LP400 and LP400S made up to 1982. Even early cars, with a 'mere' 375bhp can be good for 170mph.

> **FACT: When Countach replica kit cars became popular in the '80s urban legend had it that most stemmed from an enterprising bloke who rented a real one for the weekend, took fibreglass moulds of the body and sold them to other kit companies.**

Panther Deville

There's always the possibility that if your dad had come into a large amount of money he would have become confused by this and started thinking that he was trapped in a massive game of Monopoly. In which case he'd need an improbably styled and rather retro car with which to make his way around the board. Thankfully, between 1974 and 1985 Panther was on hand to supply just such a thing with this, the preposterous Deville.

It was meant to look like a 1930s Bugatti Royale, and from some angles that was true, provided you'd applied a generous coating of vinegar and grit to your eyes first. The interior was also meant to evoke the luxury of a bygone age, being liberally smeared in leather, whilst power came from Jaguar engines with either six or twelve cylinders. It was an extraordinary thing, as well it should have been when it cost the kind of money most people spent on a house. Little wonder that only 60 were made, nor that one of the few eager people to buy one was Elton John. Let's hope that after splashing so much cash, he didn't notice the Deville's doors were taken straight off the distinctly less expensive Austin Maxi.

★ **Years on sale:** 1974-85
★ **Engine:** straight-six cylinder, fuel-injection, 4235cc or V12 cylinder, fuel-injected, 5343cc, mounted at the front
★ **Bodywork:** four-door, four-seater saloon, six-door, six-seater limousine or two-door, four-seater convertible
★ **Top speed:** 135mph (V12)
★ **0-60mph acceleration time:** 10.5sec (V12)
★ **Maximum power:** 266bhp (V12)
★ **Original price:** £21,965

Connoisseur's choice or poverty pick? Er, well, most committed car connoisseurs would turn their noses up at this pastiche, but the very rare convertible is a magnificent beast in its own way. There was just the one limo made, finished in pink and gold…

> **FACT:** The Deville had an outing at the cinema in **The Golden Lady** starring Christina World, who was in fact called Ina Skriver but changed her name for the role so producers could say the movie starred Miss World. Badum-tish!

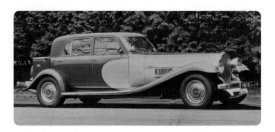

Rolls-Royce Corniche

The Rolls-Royce Corniche was a handcrafted, sumptuously appointed, whisper-quiet machine car built to the level of quality and attention you would expect from Rolls-Royce Motor Cars of Crewe. Unfortunately, a Bentley badged version also featured in the video for Elton John's bog-awful Cold War dirge, 'Nikita', and as such it's very hard to detach what was probably quite a nice car from the idea that this was a rather vulgar piece of trash for small men simpering around the place taking sinister photos of some ice-faced bint in a Russian Army uniform.

It didn't help that Elton's Corniche was in a particularly horrible red paintwork/cream leather combo that made it reminiscent of a raspberry pavlova, but even if you could put this out of your mind there was always a faint feeling that almost every Corniche was maybe a bit brash, even before the fateful moment in 1986 when Reg Dwight ruined it completely. However, if you want to avoid such a taste vacuum, you might be better off with the shorter-lived and infinitely less vulgar coupé version. Put it this way, James May off *Top Gear* has one of those. So, if you really fancy a Corniche,

here's how to work out which model you should buy. If you like flowers and throwing tantrums, get the convertible. If you like stripey jumpers and pies, don't.

★ **Years on sale:** 1971-95
★ **Engine:** V8 cylinder, single-carburettor/fuel-injected, 6750cc, mounted at the front
★ **Bodywork:** two-door, four-seater saloon or convertible
★ **Top speed:** 119mph
★ **0-60mph acceleration time:** 10.9sec
★ **Maximum power:** 225bhp (with fuel-injection)
★ **Original price:** £11,556 (Corniche saloon)

Connoisseur's choice or poverty pick? Rolls and poverty don't mix, but if it's real exclusivity you're chasing then opt for any of the Bentley alternatives to the various eras of Corniche; just that touch less flashy.

> **FACT: The Corniche's body was handmade, took five months to build and, on the convertible, featured no external seams or welds. The late Barry Sheene was quoted as saying: 'It's about the only half-decent thing Britain still makes.'**

MONEY COULDN'T BUY

Aston Martin Sotheby Special

When the Wills tobacco company wanted to promote its new line of Sotheby cigarettes, they settled on the rather lavish idea of getting Ogle Design to tear the body off an Aston Martin DBS and replace it with something unique and special. Quite a tough commission for any car stylist, but designer Tom Karen and his Ogle cohorts must have known they'd hit the spot when none other than broadcasting legend Raymond Baxter told the *Tomorrow's World* audience that the finished product was 'just about the most desirable object ever produced by the British motor industry'.

And at the time that none-more-'70s shape with its all-glass roof featuring gold strips to deflect sunlight really must have looked pretty special. One of the most remarkable features of this car, precious metal sunstrips aside, was two rows of rear lights that worked sequentially: four indicators, two reversing lights, two reflectors, and a remarkable ten brake lights, three of which on each side could shine more brightly to show following drivers how hard you were braking. It was like the Blackpool illuminations back there, just without the smell of chips.

The Sotheby Special first wowed a crowd at the 1972 Montreal

Motor Show, painted in dark blue with gold coachlines to exactly match the fag packets it was plugging. Fortunately, they didn't have bold print government health warnings back then.

★ **Year revealed:** 1972
★ **Engine:** V8 cylinder, triple-carburettor, 5340cc, mounted at the front
★ **Bodywork:** two-door, two-seater coupé
★ **Top speed:** not stated
★ **0-60mph acceleration time:** not stated
★ **Maximum power:** not stated
★ **Original price:** never on general sale

Connoisseur's choice or poverty pick? Over the years, these two bespoke Astons have changed hands a few times, so it you've set your heart on owning one then keep your eyes on *Exchange & Mart*; better look under 'Misc' as well as 'Aston Martin'.

FACT: The Sotheby smokes this car promoted were a flop but the car successfully attracted the attention of a wealthy Buckinghamshire lady who commissioned a second Ogle Aston, painted a fetching claret red. Through a succession of owners, both cars survive to this day.

Batmobile

According to the launch sequence read out by Batman's faithful boy wonder Robin in the opening 1966 TV show, the Batmobile is propelled by 'atomic batteries' and 'turbines'. Well, it wouldn't have sounded so cool if he'd solemnly intoned the real power source, 'hoary old bog-standard Ford V8 engine'. That wasn't the only slightly made-up gadgetry on board either, since this car supposedly incorporated a chain-slicer mounted in the nose, on-board phone and computer, smoke and nail spreaders to deter pursuers, and twin parachute brakes to aid instant U-turns.

The Batmobile was actually based on a mothballed 1955 Ford concept car called the Lincoln Futura, plucked from obscurity when, in summer 1965, ABC TV asked custom-car legend George Barris to create a special car for its screen incarnation of the DC Comics superhero. With just three weeks to do the job, Barris realised the old Futura in his lock-up offered a perfect starting point.

He altered the nose to resemble a bat-like facemask, flared the

Futura's already huge fins to evoke bat wings, and scalloped their trailing edges for extra menace. The concealed wheel arches were opened up, and the car's colour changed to black. The two cockpits were almost unchanged. As indeed was the engine. If only there'd been more time to fit the 'atomic batteries' and 'turbines'.

★ **Years revealed:** 1965/66
★ **Engine:** V8 cylinder, triple-carburettor, 6384cc, mounted at the front
★ **Bodywork:** two-door, two-seater roadster
★ **Top speed:** not stated
★ **0-60mph acceleration time:** not stated
★ **Maximum power:** not stated
★ **Original price:** never on general sale

Connoisseur's choice or poverty pick? The first and original Batmobile was made of metal but George Barris built three plastic copies, of which one featured in the TV show and the other two were used for publicity. In February 2007, one of the plastic ones was auctioned for £119,000.

> *FACT: The 1965 original set the style for all Batmobiles: long, dark, forbidding and with huge, bat-like rear wings. That is until the car from 2005's Batman Begins, which was supposedly inspired by a cross between a Hummer and a Lamborghini.*

Mercedes-Benz C-III

Of all the toy cars Dad inadvertently sat on as he fell wearily into the sitting-room sofa, the Mercedes C-111 must have been one of the most commonplace. Dinky, Corgi and Matchbox each made tiny scale versions of this dramatic dream car, many featuring an opening bonnet to reveal a tiny plastic reproduction of its unusual and futuristic engine: the world's first triple-rotor Wankel rotary. Sadly, although the shelves of Britain's toyshops were laden with C-111s, Dad could never hope to own a real one. They were experimental supercars as envisaged by the Germans, which meant they worked perfectly – even down to a luxurious interior with leather trim and air-conditioning – yet even a blizzard of blank cheques from wealthy fans demanding one at any price couldn't persuade Merc to put it on sale.

The first C-111 was revealed in 1969 as a rolling test-bed for rotary engine know-how, featuring a three-rotor direct fuel-injected unit, and was followed a year later by a second generation car boasting a four-rotor motor. The third evolution of the C-111 emerged years later and shunned rotary power in favour of an early experiment into turbodiesel engines. At the Nardo test track in

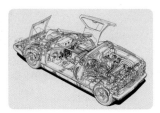

Italy it cracked 200mph and Merc continued tweaking the design until in 1979 it set the world speed record for diesel at a Germanically precise 250.958mph. The toy ones hurtled around at some speed too, at least until Dad sat on them.

★ **Year revealed:** 1969
★ **Engine:** triple- or quadruple-rotor rotary engine or straight-five 2998cc diesel/V8 4800cc petrol, fuel-injected, mounted in the centre
★ **Bodywork:** two-door, two-seater coupé
★ **Top speed:** 250mph (V8 petrol engine, C-111-IV)
★ **0-60mph acceleration time:** 4.8sec (C-111-II)
★ **Maximum power:** 500bhp (C-111-IV)
★ **Original price:** never on general sale

Connoisseur's choice or poverty pick? You can have a look at the real C-111s in Mercedes-Benz's Stuttgart museum. Or buy an old Dinky one on eBay.

> **FACT: In 1991 Merc showed the C-112, a production-ready supercar with a 6-litre V12 in the middle. But, after taking 700 deposits, they had second thoughts, triggering the biggest cashback in car industry history.**

Panther Six

In 1976, weekend television worked out a bit like this. On Saturday morning you could enjoy a repeat of Gerry Anderson's *Thunderbirds*, and marvel at Lady Penelope's wacky six-wheeled Rolls-Royce. Then on Sunday afternoon you could watch the grand prix and gasp in astonishment at the racing presence of Tyrrell's groovy six-wheeled Formula One car.

It's safe to assume that Robert Jankel, Panther chief and a former children's clothes designer, must have watched quite a bit of weekend telly in those days, because at the 1977 Earls Court Motorfair he revealed this, touted as the world's first six-wheeled road car. Not only that, it also set out to be the first standard street machine that could top 200mph. In a bitter blow to everyone who ever clapped eyes on this incredible beast, it missed both goals by miles.

One reason the whole idea fell flat was allegedly because Pirelli had second thoughts about being able to supply the mad combination of two 16-inch and four 13-inch tyres that would keep the whole car firmly planted on the road. And with a twin-turbo Caddy V8 roaring away at the back, that would have been pretty

essential. Still, before the whole project went belly up, Jankel did manage to build two real-life prototypes, both of which sort of worked. And then presumably he went back to watching telly.

★ **Year revealed:** 1977
★ **Engine:** V8 cylinder, twin-carburettor, 8193cc, mounted in the centre
★ **Bodywork:** two-door, two-seater roadster
★ **Top speed:** 200mph (claimed)
★ **0-60mph acceleration time:** 4.8sec (claimed)
★ **Maximum power:** 600bhp
★ **Original price:** not sold to the public

Connoisseur's choice or poverty pick? Two cars were built, one finished in white and the other in black. If you want to own a Panther Six, buy one of them the moment it comes up for sale or auction . . . and do let us know how it performs.

> *FACT: Had the Panther Six gone ahead it would have featured some amazing standard equipment, including a detachable hardtop, a telephone, a television and – rather worryingly – a built-in fire extinguisher.*

★ Picture Acknowledgments

The pictures used throughout this book are from the Giles Chapman Library collection and/or generously supplied by the manufacturer concerned in each case, with the following exceptions:

Alfa Romeo Montreal (left): Automobilismo Storico Alfa Romeo, Centro Documentazione.
Aston Martin DBS/V8 (left and right): LAT Photographic.
Bentley Continental S3 (left and right): WO Bentley Memorial Foundation.
Facel Vega HK500 (left and right): LAT Photographic.
Iso Grifo, (left and right): LAT Photographic.
Alfa Romeo Tipo 33 Stradale (left): Automobilismo Storico Alfa Romeo, Centro Documentazione.
Ferrari 250 GTO (left and right): LAT Photographic.
Maserati Bora (left): LAT Photographic.
Porsche 911 (left): LAT Photographic.
Ferrari 308 GTS/'Magnum' (right): Pictorial Press.